STOLEN MEMORIES

By Kathryn Fox

We lend the military our loved ones when they are at their finest and their best. They accept them willingly. They take them and they break them. When they have no more use for them, they send them home broken, without instructions on how to fix them. Only we can save them, but no one tells us how. Then we get broken too.

SYNOPSIS

A real and untold story of the cruel effects of living, loving and losing someone with Post-Traumatic Stress Disorder.

Copyright © 2013 Kathryn Fox.

The moral right of the author has been asserted.

This book is based on true events and the characters are based on real people.

Some names and places have been changed.

The book cover was designed by Kate Stone.

FOR REBECCA & DANIEL

Chapter 1 – Love at first sight

31/12/2000

I'm not looking forward to tonight; it's raining, our friends have let us down. My high hopes for a boozy New Year's Eve night out in town have seriously diminished. Still, my best friend is coming out and, if nothing else, we always have a good time together; we don't need all the others and there is still Lisa's party later. We debate whether to bother with the big open event in town or just to frequent our usual haunt, Hillsborough. But, what the heck, it's New Year's Eve, I am twenty-nine and I need to broaden my social spectrum. Hillsborough is not producing the calibre of man I want as the father of my children, so I need to look elsewhere. I have always said if I didn't have children by the time I was thirty, I would have failed. I have only ever met one man I was in love with; I worked with him when I was twenty-one; he was the boss and we had a brief fling. But he was older than me and just coming out of a marriage, so was unsure of what he wanted. We stopped it before it even started really.

I phone Alison and she agrees we should still go to town. We put our warmest clothes on, take our brollies, slap a bit of make up on, don't bother with the hair (no need – we are only going to get drenched anyway) and off we go to town.

Town is busier than I thought it might be; it's cold, wet and people are queuing at the bar. But it's New Year's Eve, I am out with my best mate and we will enjoy it. We go to the first bar and I have a pint of my favourite cider; goes down a treat – the first one always does. Alison orders a pint of cola and then quickly sneaks to the toilet to top it up with the cheap vodka in her handbag. God forbid she ever gets caught. Still, she saves a fortune.

Absolutely soaked. I look like Alice Cooper: hair drenched, eyeliner rolling down my face from my eyes. Can't cope with the cold anymore; I reckon we call it a day. Alison persuades me to go down to Hillsborough for one more, to our usual haunt; we will get in – we know the bouncers. My 'friend with benefits', Richard, will no doubt be there, so at least I am guaranteed to get a New Year's kiss or anything else I may wish to partake in.

We're in and it's packed. We get served straight away at the bar, thanks to some secretive pushing in. Off we go to our usual spot by the DJ. He's a laugh, Tom; I might have a go one day, but for now if he's not father-of-my-children material, then I might as well stick with what I know. Still, we have a cheeky kiss. I am standing on the chairs, singing along, when I see Richard. He's a bad lad, but we seem to have a thing – we have had a thing for nearly ten years now – a kind of mutual understanding: never to be a relationship, no strings, no emotions, just good no-strings 'fun'. I wave and blow him a kiss, and we give each other that knowing look; we've booked each other for later. Alison has gone off to the toilet and from my height on the chair I can see her coming back, so I climb down.

As the midnight countdown approaches, I start to make my way over to Richard, but someone pulls me back. I swing round, expecting Alison, but it's not Alison; it's some kid, looks about twelve, spots on his face, quite tall though and has a little something about him I can't put my finger on.

'Where you going?' he asks. Not that it was any of his business, but I point at Richard.

'Off to kiss that bloke,' I tell him.

'Would you prefer to kiss me?'

I decline. 'I'm nearly thirty years old; kissing kids is not my thing.'

'I'm twenty-one; how old did you think I was?'

'You look about twelve,' is my sarcastic response.

'Ten, nine, eight...' Damn, it's the ten-second countdown to the New Year and this kid is in my way. I flick a look to Richard as if to say 'I can't reach you in time'; he just laughs. Oh well, going to have to kiss this kid now; I'm not being the only one not kissing at midnight. Alison is sorted. 'Three, two, one: Happy New Year' and as 'Auld Lang's Ayne' rings out the 6ft 4 kid bends forward and kisses me. I will give him his due: he is a good kisser, so I go in for a second round.

01/01/2001

'Kathryn, Kathryn.' My lips suddenly get wrenched apart from the spotty twelve year old. It's Alison.

'Come on, we need to get to Lisa's party.' I snap back to reality.

'I'm coming.' I turn to walk away only to be grabbed again.

'Where you going?'

'To a party.'

'Am I invited? What's your name?'

'Sarah.' I always use Sarah as my get out. I got caught out once when I gave a false name and number to a guy who turned out to be the brother of one of my friends' new boyfriend. That was an awkward moment when he turned up one night and my mate introduced me as Kathryn.

'I'm Peter. What do you do for a living?'
What a boring question to ask, I think to myself.

'Nothing interesting.' I've worked at the university all my life; a good job I enjoy, but still not the most exciting.

'Do you want to know what I do?' *Not really*, I think; I really just want to get out of here, see if I can catch Richard before he goes home. Lisa won't mind if Richard comes to the party; there is a group of us that all hang out together.

'Ask me,' he says again.

'What do you do for a living?' I ask in frustration as I notice Richard leaving.

'I am in the army, I'm a soldier.' Woah, rewind. Did he just say he was in the army? How does this kid know my ideal man is a man in uniform? This changes everything. Maybe he should come to the party. Suddenly, he no longer looks twelve, albeit not twenty-one either, but still, he looks legal.

We arrive at Lisa's. Alison seems to have taken an instant dislike to Peter. Tells him he is just a kid and it's past his bedtime. He doesn't bite and just shrugs it off, tells her he likes me, so to give him a chance. He seems OK actually, quite sweet, holding my hand and putting his arm round me like we are a couple. It feels nice. We play a few games at Lisa's. I laugh at how Peter fails miserably at 'Who Wants to be a Millionaire?'. Clearly squaddies are not the brightest tools in the box. He takes the piss-take on the chin and pulls me into multiple embraces and kisses.

'He seems nice,' Lisa says. 'Looks well into you.'

'I have only just met him. Do you not think he is a bit young?'

'No,' Lisa reassures me. 'Go for it.'

It's gone 2:00 am and I am ready for home – well, Alison's. I always kip there when we go out.

'He's not coming.' Alison is still clearly not impressed with Peter. Damn, I actually think I like this kid, a lot. I give him the bad news and he goes and speaks to Alison. She seems animated, but Peter stays calm; eventually, Alison hugs him and they come over.

'OK, he can come.' We walk the short distance back to Alison's and she promptly falls asleep in front of a roaring fire as she always does.

Peter and I start to kiss and it doesn't take long before we take it upstairs. We have the most wonderful time; I have never had a night like that. Clearly he is extremely fit and whilst inexperienced he was eager to please. We must have made love all night. It was amazing. I don't think we slept; if we did, I must have dreamt of him too, because it never seemed to stop.

We finally get up and I give him a lift home. My Alice-Cooper-the-morning-after look isn't appealing so I avoid looking him dead in the eyes. I have also not taken my lenses out, so my eyes are sticky and blurred. We get to his parents' and I say goodbye. His face drops.

'Aren't you going to give me your number, Sarah?' I give it to him – the correct one – not expecting any call. I have been here before, more times than I care to mention. He gives me a kiss, which I pull back on due to having not brushed my teeth and having breath like a dog's backside.

'I will ring you later, Sarah.' Whatever, he can't even remember I gave him my real name last night. I remind him that Sarah is not my name.

'Ah, yes, it's Kathryn.' He laughs in amusement. 'You didn't look like a Sarah; Kathryn suits you better.' He lifts my chin and kisses me before climbing out of the car.

I have been home, had a wash, brushed my teeth, changed my clothes and now I am at my mum's for dinner. My sister Siobhan is there, so I tell her about last night.

'You lucky bitch,' she says. 'I went home alone.' I smile – best one night stand I ever had, if nothing else. After tea I fall asleep on the settee, last night's antics catching up with me.

'Kathryn, Kathryn, your phone's ringing,' my mum says, waking me up. Unknown number! Who's this?

'Hi, gorgeous, how are you?' I'm half-asleep so have to enquire who it is.

'It's Peter, have you forgotten me already?'

'Sorry, I was asleep.' I run outside, away from prying ears.

'I am knackered. You tired me out. Can I see you tonight?' My heart jumps.

'Yes, of course.' He agrees to come to mine at eight and we say goodbye. Short and sweet.

My phone rings again; it's my sister-in-law. I had completely forgotten I was supposed to be babysitting my seven-year-old nephew Ben at mine tonight. I try to ring Peter, but there is no answer. I pick Ben up on the way home and bring him to mine.

It's eight o'clock now and I get no answer on Peter's phone.

Nine o'clock now. He is an hour late; he must have got cold feet. Suddenly, there's a knock at the door. It's Peter.

'I'm sorry. I couldn't find you. I've been driving around for an hour.' He steps in the door and pulls me into his arms to kiss me, but I pull back. I turn around and see Ben standing there, amused by seeing his aunty about to kiss. I introduce them.

'Hello, mate.' Peter walks past me straight to Ben and shakes his hand. Ben shakes his hand back with amusement and then walks back to playing with his cars on the floor. Peter walks over, sits down with him and starts playing with the cars and talking to Ben. I shut the door to the sound of Ben's spontaneous laughter.

It's past eleven o'clock before I realise I have spent the last two hours just watching Peter play with Ben on the floor. They could go on all night. I am not sure if it's his age, but he is really good with him. Ben seems to have been in constant laughter and has never got bored with the games they've been playing. I haven't had a look in, if I'm honest, but, strangely, that hasn't mattered. I look at Peter playing with Ben and think I can see this kid making a good dad someday. Snap out of it, girl; bit too keen, you only met him yesterday. Anyway, I tell Ben it's time for bed as his mum will kill me if she finds out he has been up till this time. He gives Peter a big hug, says goodnight, then the same to me and off he goes to bed.

'Come here, you. I've missed you. I have been waiting all night to do this.' He lifts me up, lifts my chin and kisses me. I have to stand on tiptoes as he is so tall. Afterwards, we curl up on the settee wrapped in each other's arms, just kissing and staring into each other's eyes. I don't think we talked much – no need. At that moment I realise I have fallen in love with this kid I only met yesterday. We eventually go to bed and the night is as magical as it was the night before. As we lie in each other's arms, Peter lifts my head and looks me in the eyes.

'I love you.'

'You have only just met me.'

'As soon as I saw you come into the pub, with your soaking wet hair, make up running down your face, your old granny fleece on, I knew I loved you. I was at the bar. I let you push in. I followed you to the DJ. I was jealous when you kissed him. I knew I had to talk to you. I believe in love at first sight. I fell in love with you as soon as I saw you.'

I truly wanted to say it back, but I couldn't. I do believe in love at first sight, but my first sight of this kid was as a spotty twelve year old that was in my way. Love the day after doesn't have such a romantic ring to it.

Chapter 2 – Marry me?

08/01/2001

It's been a week since I met Peter and, apart from me having to go to work, we have spent every moment together. He has stayed at mine every night and I have spent every moment at work looking forward to getting home and for him to arrive. He told his family about me, who were not best impressed. They see me as some older woman just out to find a husband and whose biological clock is just ticking away. It doesn't bother me; in fact it just inspires me to prove them wrong. This has been Peter's last week of leave and he has to go back to camp tonight. We spend the whole day together. As much as I don't want him to leave, I know he has to. I'm not some eighteen year old whose life revolves around her new boyfriend. I am sure I can go a week without seeing him. After all, this time last week I had only just met him.

It's midnight.

'I have to go.' He picks up his bags from the hallway. He brought them from his parents', said goodbye to them earlier. We hold each other for a while. I feel weird; I don't want him to go. I take his bag from him to hide jokingly so that he has to stay.

'I will be home next week.' He laughs. 'Here with you, this is my home now.' That is fine by me; I want him here too. He lifts my chin

one last time and kisses me before going off
to his car.

'I love you, see you next week.' Then he
climbs into his car. *Me too*, I think but
never say. I blow him a kiss and off he
drives. I watch the lights of his car in the
distance. When they flicker away, I
spontaneously break down in tears. I feel
heartbroken; I miss him already. *Get a grip,
girl*, I tell myself and go off to bed.

09/01/2001

It's 3:30 in the morning. Beep, beep, my
phone goes with a text message. 'Back safe
in camp, can't wait to see you Friday, I love
you, Peter.' I text back 'OK'.

12/01/2001

This week has dragged so much. Spoke to
Peter for hours on the phone; going to have
to get a new contract. He will be back
tonight. I can't wait. Keep watching the
clock; hurry up. Need to get home and get
ready. He finishes at two o'clock, so will be
at mine around six, allowing for rush hour
traffic. Hurry up, clock, move faster.

Six o'clock and I made it. I have been in the
shower, re-done my make up, best
underwear on, favourite perfume on. Just
waiting for the guest of honour to arrive.

It's seven o'clock and there is no sign and
no phone call.

It's eight o'clock and there is still no sign and no phone call.

Ten o'clock now. Still no sign, no phone call. Gutted. What a mug. I should have known better at my age; should have been out with my mates tonight as well. What a prick! I decide I may as well go to bed. As I make my way upstairs, my phone rings. I hastily get it out of my pocket. Unknown number! Who's this? Can't be Peter, I have his number in my phone now so it can't be him. I say hello. 'Is that Kathryn? This is PC Smith of North Yorkshire Police. Don't panic, but Peter has been involved in an accident.' I slump on the stairs as PC Smith continues. 'Peter is OK, so don't worry, but he needs you to come and pick him up.'

'OK. Where from?' PC Smith passes the phone over.

'Hey, babe.' I hear the now familiar voice of Peter. 'Can you fetch me?'

'Are you OK?'

'Fine, yeah, can you fetch me? My car is a write off.' He gives me directions and I set off, still on auto-pilot. It can't have been too bad an accident; he sounds fine.

I find the scrap metal site fairly easily. I park up and walk past all the mangled cars and lorries. A familiar car catches my eye. It's Peter's. A wrecked, mangled mess. The front is concertinaed, the windscreen smashed and the roof is pushed down. How could anyone get out of that? It looks like it has been in a crusher. I stare at the mess when I hear a voice.

'Kathryn.' I turn and there he is, this god of a man in all his Khaki glory. He doesn't look like the spotty twelve year old I met a week ago, but a handsome, tall, heroic figure in uniform standing in front of me. I run over and throw myself into his arms. I check him for broken bones, scratches, etc.

'Don't worry, I'm fine, honest.' He laughs. I burst into tears.

'You bloody idiot. You scared me to death. Don't you know I love you and I nearly lost you? Don't ever do this to me again.'

'You love me, do you? It took you long enough to say so.'

'Well, I do, you fool, I love you.'

'Marry me then. I love you. You love me. Marry me. I want to spend my life with you. I want you to have my children. I want to be with you forever. Marry me, Kathryn.'

'Yes! Of course I will.' I scream as I jump once again into his arms and tears of joy flow this time.

13/01/2001

It's noisy outside when I wake up. For a second I forget what happened last night –

but not for long. Did I really agree to marry someone last night that I have only known for two weeks? People will think I'm mad. I look around and Peter is not in bed, but I can hear his voice. I tiptoe downstairs and I hear him talking to his nan. He has told me about his nan and granddad; they practically brought him up when his mother left and his dad then left him with them. His dad is in his life, but they don't have a great relationship. He thinks of his nan and granddad as his parents. I walk in the room just as he clicks his phone off.

'Hey, gorgeous.' He reaches forward, lifts my chin and kisses me. 'You looked so lovely sleeping I didn't want to disturb you. I have told my nan, granddad, dad and stepmum we are getting married and they want to meet you. We can go round tonight.' *Woah, slow down, mate*, I think. This is going too fast.

'I can't tonight. I am out with the girls; it's been planned for ages.'

'Tomorrow then. I will drop you off tonight and go and see them. Ring me and I will pick you up; I want you home safe.' Wow, thought he would be pissed off I was going out. How great is this man.

It's nearly midnight as I climb into my car. I lent it to Peter seeing as his has been turned to mush. I lurch forward and give him a big drunken kiss.

'I missed you, I love you,' I say, slurring my speech.

'Good night?' He laughs.

'Yes and no. Good, but I wanted to get home to you. I love you,' I say again. 'Did you have a good night without me?' His face drops. He missed me loads obviously.

'I went to see my family. They spent all night lecturing me about you. They reckon it won't last, it's too fast and it would end in a few months anyway before I go to Cyprus.' He has mentioned Cyprus; he is being posted there in October for two years. October seems so far away I haven't really thought that far ahead.

'You will just have to marry me before you go to Cyprus; that will show them.' Clearly the drink has taken over my senses.

'Let's do it. Why not? I don't want to wait anyway.'

'OK.' I am clearly not really thinking straight. I will have forgotten this in the morning.

14/01/2001

What a hangover! I curl into Peter's side and wake him in the process.

'I'm dying.'

'I have no sympathy.' He laughs. 'You need to get yourself together; don't forget we are going to my nan's today.' Oh great, I had forgotten that. That's all I need: the tenth degree from an overprotective granny who thinks I am some hormonal ticking time bomb who has ensnared this young lad. I make a feeble attempt to make him stay in bed with me instead.

'You will be fine. When they meet you they will love you. Just as much as I do.' I curl up again in his arms and grab another hour before I have to get ready to leap into the lion's den.

Peter knocks on the door. Why am I so nervous? I am a twenty-nine-year-old intelligent woman; I shouldn't be worried by a couple of pensioners. The door opens and Peter's granddad, Ken, opens the door.

'Come in, son.' Peter shakes his granddad's hand. *How very grown up*, I think. 'Your nan's in the room with your mum and dad.' Damn, I didn't realise it was the full firing squad all at once. Ken beckons me in. 'Come in, love, go through.' I follow him through into the room. His nan, dad and stepmum say hello to us both and we sit down. Silence. Ken asks if I want tea.

'Yes, please, one sugar.' He takes the rest of the orders and off he pops with Peter's nan, Margaret, closely following. They leave the rest of us together.

'So, when you getting married?' Clearly this is a sarcastic dig at my expense from Francis, Peter's stepmum. *Bitch*, I think. I tell her, 'Before he goes to Cyprus.' That should shut her up. 'September then, better buy my hat.' Another dig. Peter's dad, Sean, doesn't say much. Clearly there is tension between him and Peter. I'll ask him later. We have tea and make small talk. Actually they're OK; Francis is only a few years older than me so we actually have a lot in common. His dad is an odd one; I can't really work him out or what the problem is between him and Peter. Clearly Peter sees his grandparents as his parents and it shows.

We stay a couple of hours before making our excuses. When we get home I quiz Peter about the hostility between him and his dad.

'Mum and Dad were alcoholics. They never looked after me and my sister. My mum took her when she left; she didn't want me so she left me at school. My nan and granddad came and picked me up from school; I was about seven at the time. I barely saw my dad. He would come and go when he wanted and was always an arsehole. I promise I will never be like him. I will be the best dad you can imagine to our children; I will never abandon or hurt them like he did to me. My kids will always come first. You and my kids will mean everything to me. I don't want to wait to have children. I want you to be pregnant as soon as possible.'

He was so sincere. I could actually see this happening. Even contemplating having a baby was amazing; my only ambition in life was to be a mum, so to be talking about the real possibility felt so right. We start practising immediately.

Later that night I have to give him a lift to meet his mates. As his car is a write off, he has to get a lift back to camp. A pal who lives in Barnsley has agreed to pick him up en route. I turn the engine on and we set off. The CD playing in the stereo is Shania Twain. I don't buy much music to be honest, but I do like Shania. 'From this moment, life has begun…' starts to ring out. Peter reaches forward and turns the sound up.

'I like this song,' he says. 'It's about me and you. It will be our first dance song.' Sweet; I laugh at this 6ft 4 squaddie singing along to a sloppy love song. I fall in love with him a little bit more with every second that passes. Before the song has a chance to finish for the second time we're at the meeting point and his mates are waiting. Time for one last kiss.

'Put her down,' I hear from the car full of his mates.

'You're just jealous, you dicks.' He turns to me. 'I love you.'

'I love you too.' Then he's gone.

Chapter 3 – Rebecca

15/03/2001

The last couple of months have whizzed by. Peter has met all my family now and they all love him, my friends as well, especially Alison; she thinks the sun shines out of his backside now. How very different from when they first met. He is very good with her young daughter, Laura; she sees him as a bit of an honorary stepdad. We have an appointment today at the register office to book our wedding. We are definitely hoping for some time in September. Peter is off to Sierra Leone for six weeks at the end of July so we are planning it for when he comes back. His departure to Cyprus has been postponed till the following March now, so we have a little longer together before he goes. We get to the register office on time and all goes smoothly, 29th September 2001 is booked. Peter will have to get permission from the army to marry me, but it won't be a problem; it's not like I am some terrorist.

13/7/2001

I can't believe how happy I am; life could not be any better. Peter has a couple of weeks of leave before he departs for Sierra Leone. We are curled up on the sofa when our conversation turns to children. We have discussed it several times before. We are planning to start seriously trying for a baby as soon as we are married; but Peter is keener than that.

'I can't wait. We should start trying now. We will be married before the baby arrives.'

'You go away in two weeks. It's not that simple.'

I have just finished my period, so we agree that I will stop taking the pill. I have heard it takes a couple of months for the pill to be out of your system so by the time he gets back from Sierra Leone and we get married, it should actually fall right.

25/7/2001

It's the night before Peter goes off to Sierra Leone; I can't believe I won't see him for six weeks. Whilst we only see each other at weekends and when he is on leave, six weeks seems such a long time. He popped out earlier without me, didn't know where he went. We are sat in the living room when he suddenly reaches for his bag.

'Don't think me mad, but I bought this.' From his bag he produces a pregnancy test. 'I just want to know before I go away.'

'You fool. It's too soon; I won't be pregnant.' To put his mind at rest I pop upstairs to do the test. I know it will be negative and, no surprise, it is. I go downstairs and tell him. He looks gutted, bless him. We snuggle up in each other's arms; he has to leave at

midnight to go back to camp. He is leaving
his new car here and a mate is picking him
up. They will leave camp at six o'clock
heading for Brize Norton and will fly out at
twelve. We are so comfortable we fall asleep
in each other's arms. Knock, knock,
knock... Damn, it's midnight and his
friends are knocking. Peter goes to the door
and tells his mate to give him a minute. He
comes back and scoops me up. My tears
start to roll. He tells me not to cry as I will
set him off. He lifts my chin and kisses me.
It leads to the quickest but most emotional
sex I have ever had and then he is gone.

15/8/2001

It's been three weeks now since Peter went
away. He rings when he can – not often
enough for my liking. I carry on with my
daily routine. It's Friday and me and my
colleague Fiona always go to the pub
opposite work on Friday for lunch and a
quick half-pint.

'Cajun chicken baguette and half a cider?'
Anne, the landlady, asks.

'Of course.'

I have the same every week. Fiona says,
'Make that two.' We chat about work. How
sad are we! Peter rings my mobile whilst I
am there. We talk briefly about the wedding
and how my Cajun baguette seems a little
undercooked, but it might just be me. I eat
it anyway. Fiona and I go back to work and

then another week is done. I spend the weekend making arrangements for the wedding. All pretty much booked now. Think the Cajun chicken has come back to haunt me as I have a dodgy stomach all weekend.

18/8/2001

Another Monday morning. I still feel dodgy. I ask Fiona if she has been OK after the Cajun chicken and she says she has. She says mine did look a little dodgy. I get through the routine of the week. Peter rings every day and we talk about the wedding. His regiment are staying out there a little longer than expected, but he will return on special leave on 11th September. He won't come home until the 28th, the day before the wedding, but as long as he is here for the 29th, that's all that matters. On Friday, I make an appointment at the doctors' because I still don't feel well. It can't be the chicken. On my way home I stop off at the pharmacy to pick up some bits for the house. Whilst I am there something seems to catch my eye and resonates with something Fiona had said due to me feeling sick.

'Are you pregnant?'

I said 'no' as we did the test before he went away so I can't be. Then I remember. Surely the quickie whilst his mates waited outside couldn't have got me pregnant. I am actually late. I buy a test on the off-chance.

I don't think I am, but I suppose the doctor will ask me later so I might as well just make sure. I run upstairs when I get home – got to be quick. I only have half an hour till the doctors'. I wee on the little stick and put it on the side and go and get changed. I come back just to check I am not pregnant... a blue line... really... I stare at it from different angles; is it really? I try to convince myself it's not, but it is: I'M PREGNANT. Oh my god, oh my god... really... really... I start crying with such joy. I ring Alison first; she is at work and she shouts it out to all her colleagues. Then I ring my sister – she cries; then my mum, Peter's stepmum, nan, etc; everyone I can apart from the one person I want to share it with but who I can't contact.

25/8/2001

It's been a week now since I found out I am pregnant and I have not been able to tell Peter as he is 'out in the field'. But tonight he rings.

'It's me. I miss you so much. What you up to? You having a drink with the girls tonight?'

'No, I can't.'

'Why not?'

'Because I'm pregnant.' Silence. 'Are you there?'

'Yes. Really or are you winding me up?' I confirm it's true. 'Jacko, Jacko, I am going to be a dad.' I hear big cheers and shouts of 'well done, lad' in the background. Jacko is one of his best mates. They have been together since they both joined, brothers in arms and all that.

'Babe, I have to go. We are back out on manoeuvres and won't be back until 10th September and then I fly home in the early hours on the 11th. I love you and my baby. Please take care of him or her. I don't care what it is. But take care of my baby. I am the luckiest, happiest man alive,' he says. 'Thanks to you. I love you so much, I can't wait to get home and marry you and meet my baby. Take care and I will see you soon.'

'Bye, my love.' Then he is gone.

11/09/2001

My future husband returns today. He rang me earlier; one of his friends is going home and lives in Durham and is going to drop him off at home so he can pick his car up. He can't stay; he has to set off straight back as he is on duty in the morning, but at least we get an hour together. Fancy that: a three and a half hour drive either way just to spend an hour with me. He must really love me and our child growing inside me. In my day dreaming of looking forward to him coming, I don't hear my mobile ringing; it's Mum. *What's she want?* I think; probably ringing to moan about my dad. I ignore her and let it ring off. My work phone then rings so I have to answer; it's Mum. She sounds upset.

'Have you seen the news?' Why would I? I'm at work. 'A plane has flown into the twin towers in New York and as they were filming the flames another one flew into the second tower. It's awful.' I run upstairs to the staff room and flick on the TV. Oh my god, she is not kidding. I watch in awful silence as I see one, then two planes fly into the towers. It is shown over and over again. The staff room quickly fills up with other members of staff. I find myself still there after an hour. My boss comes to find me and tells me to go home and not to let this upset me as well as to look forward to Peter coming home and the wedding. I pack my stuff and set off home.

My phone rings. It's Peter. He is about twenty minutes away. Those twenty minutes seem to take forever, but then the door swings open and in he comes. My hero, in his uniform, looking so strong and powerful, certainly no longer the spotty twelve year old I first met, but my true soul mate and the love of my life. I am sat down and he lifts me up, lifts my chin and kisses me. Then he kneels down, holds my hips with one hand and lifts my top with the other; he leans forward and kisses my belly.

'Hello, you in there. You don't know this, but I love you and I can't wait to see you.' He then looks up at me but continues talking to my belly. 'Your mummy has made me the happiest man alive and I love her so very much.' He kisses my tummy again and strokes it. 'I will see you soon, baby.' He stands back up taking me in his arms, lifting my chin, and kisses me again. I break suddenly to ask him if he has seen the news and what has gone off in New York; he says 'yes', but dismisses it as it doesn't affect us. I feel a very quick chill run through me; how could I have ever known that the knock-on effects of what happened on that day, thousands of miles away, would ultimately take him from me in the most unimaginable way and destroy our love forever.

29/9/2001

Bleep, bleep, my alarm goes off. I roll over and switch off the alarm. As I roll back, I see it. My wedding dress. Of course, it's my WEDDING DAY. I reach for my mobile and ring Peter; he answers straight away.

'Did I wake you?'

'No, I have been awake for ages. Couldn't sleep, I am so excited.'

'Me too.' I hear my mum shout as it's time to go to the hairdressers. 'Got to go, babe. I will see you at 12:00 noon at the register office.'

'I hope so.' He laughs. We both say 'I love you' and off I go to the hairdressers.

I arrive at the register office with ten minutes to spare. I can see all my family and friends. I can't see Peter. Alison tells me he is here, he just went inside to check everything was OK. The rest of my friends arrive and I meet and greet them all. One of them taps my shoulder; I spin round and it's him. He is in his mess dress with all the tassels and his peaked cap. His medals prominently displayed. He looks so handsome. He lifts my chin and kisses me.

'You ready to marry me then, Miss Casey?'

'Yes.'

'Then let's go.' He takes my hand and leads me inside, followed by all our family and friends. The ceremony is very swift; before we know it we are pronounced man and wife. Wow, what a whirlwind; nine months ago we met and here we are married and with a baby on the way. The rest of the day is so wonderful; we have our reception with family and close friends, and then a big party for extended family and friends. At nine o'clock it's time for the first dance. We take our positions on the dance floor and the music begins. 'From this moment, life has begun, from this moment you are the one, right beside me...' What else could it be. We lose ourselves in each other on the dance floor; there is no one else there. As the last few words ring out, Peter leans in, lifts my chin and kisses me.

'I love you, Mrs Fox.'

25/12/2001

It's CHRISTMAS. Our first Christmas together and my first Christmas when I can't have a beer or two. I am over five months pregnant now and not someone who is hiding it well. Luckily, Peter doesn't drink anyway, so I don't feel like I am missing out. It's our first Christmas and we spend it together, just me, Peter and the bump. I wouldn't want it any other way.

31/12/2001

'Happy anniversary, Mrs Fox.' To the second. Gosh, how did he remember that? One year since we met on that rainy, miserable night. This last year has been the most amazing ride of my life. All my dreams have come true within the space of twelve months. 'Here's to the next twelve months, Mrs Fox.' We toast the New Year with a clink of our cups of tea.

11/03/2002

I am used to the absences now. It's part of being an army wife. The week-long absences are OK, but the impending two-year posting to Cyprus is drawing near. He goes on 25th March and our baby is due on 4th April, so unless we can make him or her come early, it is pretty guaranteed that he won't be here for the birth. Peter is on pre-deployment leave. We try all the old wives' tales to try and make the baby come early. Nothing works, not even a twinge. How disappointing. But I take it on the chin, army wife and all that; the army and duty come first.

24/03/2002

Here we are again, another goodbye as he has to leave for work. But this one is different. This is tinged with sadness and joy. I don't know when we will see each other again, but I do know that when we do we will have a new baby son or daughter. He has been told he can come back when the baby is born, but can't have time off for the birth. We hug; he lifts my chin and kisses me, and then kisses my now enormous swollen belly.

'You take care of your mummy, you hear. I will see you both very, very soon. I love you, little one. I love you, Kathryn.' We embrace again and he is gone. This time to Cyprus.

11/04/2002

I am so bored. I am on maternity leave now. My due date has been and gone. No twinges or anything. If one more person rings me and asks me if I feel anything, I will scream. Seven days overdue now and no sign at all. I am booked in to be induced on the 15th so only four more days at the most. My boss rings from work to see how I am. They are struggling to get some stats together for a meeting so I offer to go in. He tries to talk me out of it, but I insist – got nothing better to do. I get in to work and sort out the stats, takes about an hour, but I am glad of having something to do. I take the ten-minute walk, or should I say waddle, over to the Finance Director's office to drop off the report and then I head home.

It's late. Eleven o'clock. Peter rings.

'Hi, babe. I know it's late, but just checking in before I go to bed. You OK?' I tell him I am fine and just getting ready for bed myself. We talk for about an hour and then say our goodbyes. I pick up my cup and plate. I had some garlic bread before he rang and head for the kitchen. As I reach the door I am stopped in my tracks by the most unusual and weird pain in my stomach. My mum warned me it would feel like this; it's a contraction. It eases off and I go to the kitchen. Arrghh, again there it is. I ring Peter.

'Babe, it's started and it bloody hurts.'

'Ring Mick.' Mick is my brother, who is on standby to take me to hospital. 'Please, babe, don't wait.'

'OK. I will let you know what's happening.'

'I love you and give my baby a kiss for me when they get here.'

12/04/2002

After a bout of throwing up, which made the delivery room stink of garlic, a desperate begging for an epidural, a weird spaced out feeling after massive consumptions of gas and air, I give birth to a 7lb 14oz baby girl. Debbie, my sister-in-law and birth partner, is crying and the midwives are in awe of how perfect she is. The cord is round her neck so it is a second or two before she is placed on my chest. She is without question the most beautiful thing I have ever seen. She is beyond perfect. I am a brutally honest person and if a baby is ugly, I say so, but this gorgeous baby girl is more than I could ever have hoped for or imagined. She is perfect in every single way. How did I produce something so absolutely amazingly beautiful as this little angel laid on my chest?

'Do you have a name for her?'

'Rebecca.'

'What a beautiful name for a beautiful girl.' The midwives take her away to clean her up. Debbie comes and gives me a hug; she is still crying.

'I will go and ring your mum and get Mick to pick me up.' She goes outside. The midwife brings Rebecca back all wrapped up and clean.

'Here you go, Mummy.' She leaves us alone for a minute. Just me and my beautiful baby girl. I just stare in amazement and know that I will love and protect this precious little bundle for the rest of my life. The love you feel for your first child is the most wonderful feeling ever. I lean forward and kiss her forehead.

'That is from your daddy. He loves you very much and will love and protect you forever. You are a very lucky girl, you know, to have such a wonderful daddy who has waited for you all his life. You and me are the luckiest girls alive.'

We only get a few moments together before the visitors start to arrive; my mum first, then Peter's stepmum and dad. His dad walks in with his mobile phone to his ear. He passes me the phone and promptly whisks Rebecca out of my mum's arms. I say hello, expecting Peter's nan.

'Hello.' A male voice. 'I'm a dad, babe.'

'I know, love.' I am annoyed that his dad did not allow me to be the one to tell him.

'Babe, I can't believe it. I can't stop crying. What's she like? Does she look like me? She does as it goes, poor thing.'

'She is perfect, Peter, she is so beautiful, we did well, my dear.'

'You did. I am so proud of you. I wish I had been there. I will be home soon to see you both. I love you both so very much.' I am off to the ward so he agrees to ring later and off me and my entourage go to the ward.

Francis has Rebecca now and carefully
carries her whilst I am wheeled in a chair –
very embarrassing.

Chapter 4 – Cyprus

26/04/2002

Two weeks since my beautiful little girl was born and today her daddy is coming home to see her for the first time. He landed at Brize Norton about an hour ago. Should be here around eleven o'clock. He rings to tell me there has been an accident on the M1 and he is still at least an hour and a half away.

'Please wait up for me.' I try, but, unfortunately, having a newborn baby means you don't get much choice in the times you manage to get to sleep and I drop off. I awake from a brief but welcome sleep by someone stroking my hair and kissing my forehead. It's Peter. I never heard him come in.

'I have been here for ten minutes just watching you sleep.' I notice he has Rebecca in his arms.

'I see you have met your daughter.'

'I have. She is be—' He can't finish his sentence as a lump comes into his throat and tears stream down his face. It is clearly overwhelming for him. He lies down on the settee with me and places Rebecca between us. We lie there for a while, just absorbing our happy little family unit. I can't imagine how life could get any better than this.

10/05/2002

The last two weeks have flown by. Peter has rarely put Rebecca down. He's very hands on: changing nappies, feeding her, bathing her. Very protective, has to be forced to pass her over otherwise he would never let her go. Clearly a daddy's girl already. I don't mind suddenly being the second most important lady in his life. He has to return to Cyprus tomorrow, leaving tonight for Brize Norton. It won't be for too long though. Rebecca and I are going over there for six months whilst I am on maternity leave. We have managed to sort out a house on camp. I'm not looking forward to being a PAD wife though, not my thing, but looking forward to being able to see Peter every day. We have not experienced that yet.

12/06/2002

The plane lands at RAF Akrotiri in Cyprus. The official ushers me forward as I am carrying Rebecca in the car seat and he helps carry my bags into the airport. I wait for my luggage and again the official helps me and pushes the trolley through the arrivals lounge. As we come through the door, Peter is waiting for us. His face lights up as he sees us and he runs towards us. He whisks Rebecca off me and leaves me to take over the reins of the trolley; *thanks, love*, I think. He realises what he has done, puts Rebecca down and lifts me up into a passionate embrace. He puts me down and promptly takes over pushing the trolley and carrying Rebecca. He is so strong now. We take the two-hour scenic route through Cyprus to Dhekelia where he is posted. It feels so surreal. I can't actually believe I am here. We get to the house. It's nothing to shout home about, really basic, but still it's only for six months, not like I intend to make it my home for ever. We go to a lovely restaurant overlooking the sea that first night. I was wrong: things can get better. Here I am, looking out over a clear blue sea, with my handsome husband and my gorgeous little girl. I feel so lucky.

13/06/2002

My first full day in Cyprus: Peter went off to work at 6:00 am, but will be home in a minute for lunch. He is going to take me down to the Battalion private beach. His car pulls up and he gets out the driver's side. The passenger side swings open and another tall, strapping squaddie strides out. A handsome lad with blond hair and piercing blue eyes. Peter introduces him.

'This is Jacko.'

This is the infamous Jacko I have heard so much about or James to give him his Sunday name. He kisses me on the cheek and asks if he can hold Rebecca. All four of us go to lunch. James plays with Rebecca constantly, only stopping to fetch her a starfish from the sea. I am surprised that Peter lets him without wanting to have her all to himself. They clearly have a very special bond between them, him and Jacko. After lunch they drop me off back at the house and off they go back to work. I don't wait up for Peter that night as he is going to be late. As I settle in bed, I suddenly here the thunder of a plane going overhead – that was low. I run to the window to see the biggest military plane I have ever seen. Of course, I remember, Cyprus is within striking distance of Iraq. The two wars in Iraq and Afghanistan are right on my doorstep now even though earlier by the beach they seemed a million miles away. Peter is due to go to Iraq in November for six weeks. I will have returned to England by then.

25/08/2002

We are sat in a karaoke bar enjoying the horrendous singers, when James and some of the other squaddies come in. Clarky is another of Peter's best friends and he, Peter and James seem to be the three musketeers. It's Clarky's last night though as he is leaving the army. James is always up at the house and seems to have fallen in love with Rebecca; mind you, who could blame him and she has clearly taken a shine to him. He goes up to the DJ and puts in his request. He is a really good singer actually. Not like Peter. They sing some daft songs together, all three of them, which has everyone laughing; but then James will get up and sing properly. He beckons me over to the DJ box next to the stage. I have Rebecca in my arms and go over.

'Give her here.' I entrust my precious bundle to him and return to my seat next to Peter.

'What's he doing?' Peter puts his arm around me.

'I have no idea.'

James climbs on the stage with Rebecca in one arm and the mic in the other. There is a collective 'ahh' in the room as he plants a kiss on her cheek. They stare into each other's eyes in mutual admiration. The music starts and James's beautiful voice rings out.

'Baby, can I hold you tonight? Baby, if I told you the right words... you'llbe mine...' Another Boyzone classic. He sings the whole song to Rebecca as if they are the only two people in the room. I can see all the single girls in the room swooning and trying to catch his eye, but he has eyes for only one girl: Rebecca. As he finishes, the whole bar cheers and claps, the loudest I have heard tonight. It makes Rebecca jump and she gets a little frightened. James hands the mic back to the DJ and protectively snuggles Rebecca into his neck; she instinctively wraps her arms around him for comfort. He carries her back and Peter stands up to take her. The only man she loves more than James is Peter. She has calmed down and James gives her a kiss and passes her back to Peter. He is off to the club with Clarky. He kisses me goodbye and off he goes.

'Why don't you go with them? I can take Rebecca home.'

'No. I prefer to be with you and Rebecca. I am not a single bloke; I shouldn't be out with them when I have a beautiful wife and child I could be with.' I don't know if it's being a squaddie that makes him hold his family so dear or the fact that he never had a secure and loving family unit of his own when he grew up. He often tells me how he wants his kid's life to be different to the one he had.

07/11/2002

The months have flown by. I am going home a little earlier, as Peter leaves for Iraq on the 10th. We have made the two-hour journey back to RAF Akrotiri. James has tagged along for the journey. We are a bit late actually so don't have much time before we need to board the plane. James says his goodbyes and leaves us for some time alone. As we get to the boarding gate I hand in my tickets. I dread turning round as I know what I am going to face; but it has to be done. I turn and, yes, Peter has Rebecca's head cradled to his and he has tears tumbling down his cheeks.

'I don't want you both to go. I may never see you again.'

'Don't talk like that. I know you will be fine. You have to be. We need you back.' He passes Rebecca to me and cradles us both in his big strong arms. We try and make it last forever, but then the last call comes for the plane. We have to go. He lifts my chin and gives me one last kiss before I walk away. I try not to look back, but I do and then my tears fall.

10/11/2002

It's late and my phone is ringing. At this time it can only be one person.

'It's me, babe. I am just waiting to get the plane for Iraq. I don't know when I will get to ring again. I wanted to tell you I love you and Rebecca more than anything in the world. I will think of you both every day and that will keep me strong. I love you both.'

'You do that. We want you home in one piece. We love you.' Then he is gone.

24/12/2002

Christmas Eve and I am at Stansted Airport; Peter is back today. They arrived back in Cyprus yesterday evening and he went straight to Larnaka Airport and waited hours before he could get a flight home to us. The plane landed half an hour ago so he should not be long now. The doors open and people start streaming out with their luggage. Eventually we see him and he sees us; he runs over to the barrier and whisks Rebecca from my arms and holds her in the air. The security guards look amused; they shouldn't really have let him, but they can see he is no danger and just wants to hold his daughter. We walk either side of the barriers until the exit where we can all hug each other officially.

25/12/2002

Rebecca's first Christmas. I am not sure she knows what is going on. Our cat, Spooky, seems more interested in the presents. But eventually she gets into the spirit, with ample encouragement from her daddy. We have gone to town on her to be honest; the room looks like Santa's grotto. Peter helps Rebecca open all her presents. I step back a little as he won't get to have a lot of moments like this with her and I want him to experience as much as he can. After all, she is Daddy's girl.

06/01/2003

We had pushed it to the back of our minds, but yet again here we are saying our goodbyes. Peter has to return to Cyprus today. His dad is taking him back to the airport. That's a novelty: his dad doing something for him. The journey will no doubt be a silent one. This goodbye does not actually seem so bad as the good news is that he is returning in March for six months on a course so he will be home in a few months and we will see him every weekend. His dad is here so we go through our regular routine of goodbyes and 'I love you' and off he goes, again.

11/09/2003

It's been two years now since the planes flew into the twin towers. I still remember that day clearly, although with happiness. I recall that was the first time I had seen Peter since I told him I was pregnant with Rebecca. The war in Afghanistan was still raging on, although the aftermath seems to be worse than the actual battle itself. I read a really sad piece in the paper recently where it talked about the invisible injury, something called Post-Traumatic Stress Disorder (PTSD). A squaddie who had been involved in the first Gulf War had come back suffering from PTSD. He had been a loving father and husband when he went away, but came back violent and abusive. His wife couldn't cope and left him and took the kids. She let him have them one day and he promptly took them out into the woods and slit their throats before hanging himself. Such a tragedy. The poor woman. Luckily, as Peter's regiment were in Cyprus, they were not going to be deployed any time soon.

1/12/2003

Wow, this year is whizzing by. I am so glad; only three months till Peter returns for good. He has been on the course and back to Cyprus, but comes back today for Christmas leave. We go to Manchester this time to pick him up. Rebecca is over a year and a half now, running around everywhere. She spots him before I do and nips under the barrier. This time the security guards are not so nice and shout at her to go back. She turns tail and runs back to me crying. Peter shouts at the guards and they tell him to watch his mouth. I catch Peter's eye and motion to leave it. Whilst I can see it's a struggle, as he naturally wants to protect his child, he walks away to us where Rebecca can safely run into his arms.

'Hello, princess. Have you missed me?'

'Yes. Mummy missed you too.'

'Has she? How much?'

'This much.' She demonstrates by extending her arms as far as she can.

'That's good enough for me.' He lifts my chin and plants one of those wonderful kisses on my lips. That night in bed, with Rebecca asleep between us, he looks me in the eye.

'I want another baby. A son.' So for the second time we start practising.

23/12/2003

Déjà vu strikes again and we are preparing our goodbyes as he returns to Cyprus; but we are on the last stretch. He will return for good on 27th February. As he leaves the last thing he says is to do a test. I was true to my word and we had tried to get pregnant with a boy. We did all the old wives' tales; but it was too soon to do a test so I promised I would do one in a week.

31/12/2003

New Year's Eve. Three years now since Peter and I met. Amazing. I bought a test yesterday, but thought I would wait till today so I can ring Peter on the anniversary of when we met to tell him I was pregnant with his son. I hadn't done the test yet, but I had a good feeling. I go upstairs and wee on the stick. This time I watch in anticipation, expecting the blue line. It doesn't appear at first, but then slowly and faintly I can see the line. I check it over and over, squint my eyes a bit, but it is there, albeit not as vibrant as it was with Rebecca. I am pregnant again. I run for my phone and ring Peter. He answers, expecting me.

'I'm pregnant!'

'With my son?'

'Of course.' A son would just make everything so complete. I hear the familiar shout again to Jacko that he is going to be a dad again. I hear the phone being wrenched from Peter's hands.

'Congratulations, Mrs Fox. Can I be godfather?'

'Of course.' I have a little chat with James before he sidelines me and asks to speak to his little girlfriend. He speaks to her often if he is there when Peter rings. I hand Rebecca the phone.

'James, James, James,' she squeals down the phone. She gets into deep conversation before she hands the phone back. 'James gone.' She looks sad. Peter is back on the phone, amused that when he came on she passed it back. We chat for a while prematurely about names for our son, never contemplating it may be a girl. Before I know it an hour has passed, Rebecca is asleep and I had better go to bed. 'Speak soon,' we say and off we go to our respective beds thousands of miles apart.

27/02/2004

He's home. Well, I say home, the regiment is back from Cyprus and have arrived at their new barracks in Edinburgh. They will spend a few months settling in before they get some well-earned leave. Peter will be home at weekends though, a four-hour drive either way. I worry about him driving that far every weekend, but he tells me he would drive ten hours either way if it meant spending an hour or two with me and

Rebecca. I feel so blessed to have such a devoted husband. Clearly me, Rebecca and our unborn child mean the world to him.

Chapter 5 – Daniel

19/05/2004

It's an exciting day today. I am going for my twenty-week scan. They have changed the policy in Sheffield and you can now ask for the midwife to tell you the sex of your baby. We definitely want to know. We are desperate for it to be a boy. Peter has managed to wangle the extra day off work to come with me. That's a miracle in itself as the army very rarely gives the guys any time off for domestic issues. We get to the hospital in plenty of time, but still have to wait an hour for my name to be called. Finally, they call my name and in we both go. Rebecca is at her nan's so it's just the two of us. The cold gel is squirted on my tummy and the sonogram moved side to side. I hear the familiar 'buum buum, buum buum'; my baby's heartbeat is clear and strong. The midwife talks us through the white skeletal figure on the screen, 'That's your baby's head, their arms, legs, etc. The heart is there pumping strong.' She takes the necessary measurements and confirms everything is in order and then asks if we want to know what sex it is. I look at Peter and we both say 'yes' at the same time. She runs the sonogram across my tummy and I can see on the screen she is focussing between my baby's legs. I can't make head nor tail of it myself; don't know how they figure it out. She smiles to herself having clearly worked it out. She doesn't say straight away; she wipes the gel off my tummy and pulls my top back down.

'Well, I am happy to tell you, you are going to have a new baby BOY. Is that what you wanted?' *Oh my god*, I think, *you don't know how much.*

'Yes.' I turn to look at Peter again. He has a single tear trickling down his cheek. 'Happy?'

'Happy. Thank you so much. I love you.' He lifts my chin to plant one of those favourite kisses of mine. He then addresses my tummy. 'Hi, son.'

05/07/2004

Peter is back in camp safely. He has just finally had his three weeks' leave after they returned from Cyprus. We spent it doing Daniel's room. We settle on Daniel as a name for our son; Daniel Peter Fox to be exact. Peter is keen for him to have his name as well; says he wants everyone to know he is his. He rings late.

'Jacko is in deep shit. I have just spoken to him. He hasn't even set off yet from Plymouth and we are on parade at 0600 in the morning. It's about an eight-hour drive from Plymouth to Edinburgh so he will be cutting it fine.' Jacko is a good lad and is so proud and excited that he is going to be Daniel's godfather, though he is a bit of a boy racer, unfortunately, so he no doubt thinks he will make it. Peter used to be the same, but after his crash when we first met he started to drive sensibly and made sure he left in plenty of time, plus he was a dad now and had to be more sensible.

06/07/2004

Peter rings me at work.

'Morning, babe. Just finished fitness. Jacko's still not here. He is in a whole world of shit.' I hear a voice in the background telling Peter he needs to get back on parade asap. 'I have to go; I will call you back in a bit.'

My phone rings again; it's Peter, true to his word he has phoned me back – didn't think he meant this quick.

'Kathryn. Jacko is DEAD. He's DEAD. He was killed in a car crash this morning returning to camp. They have just told us on parade. They have told me to take some time out before going back to work.' The tears pour from my eyes at my desk. My colleagues clearly realise something is up as the office goes silent. Peter goes silent. I ask if he is OK, but clearly he is devastated and can hardly speak. I tell him to ring me in a bit.

'OK.' He is clearly choked up. I put the phone down and burst into tears, telling my colleagues what has happened. They tell me to go home. I go, but to my mum's where Rebecca is and I break down there. How can we tell Rebecca?

09/07/2004

Jacko's funeral takes place today. Typical army, they took over and made all the arrangements, bussed the lads down from Edinburgh and wouldn't let Peter make his own way there so he could pick me up en route. I am heavily pregnant now with Daniel and can't make my own way there so I have to miss it. Peter will carry the coffin along with some of the other lads. He took Jacko's number two to the funeral parlour last night so they could dress him in it. A few of his closest friends went round to meet his parents yesterday. Peter had never met them before, but they knew all about him, even knew about Rebecca. Apparently he talked about her a lot and how much he thought of her. They even produced a picture of them at the house in Cyprus. It was a lovely picture of Jacko laid back on the settee with Rebecca curled up on his chest. I had always wondered where that picture went. They gave it to Peter to bring home for her. We decide not to tell Rebecca he has been killed; she is only two and it would be too upsetting. The funeral goes well, in fact, in true regimental tradition choreographed perfectly. Peter rings on the coach back to camp; he is very subdued and, of course, extremely sad. We don't say much, but Peter has a question to ask.

'Babe, would you mind if we give Daniel an additional name?' I don't mind at all. I know what he is thinking. 'Daniel Peter JAMES Fox. I want to pay tribute to him in a lasting way. He was my best mate and I miss him.' I sense he is about to crumble so I let him go. He is on the coach and any sign of weakness is frowned upon by the army and he would be told to man up.

18/09/2004

It's my mum's sixtieth birthday today and we are having a party at my brother's house. I drive down there, uncomfortable and the size of a house. I am five days overdue now. Why do none of my children want to come on time? Mind you, Peter is in Ireland at the moment, but is home in three days, so if I hang on till then he will be at the birth. I hope he is. He missed out on Rebecca being born and we don't intend to have any more. Now that we are having a boy our little family will be complete. I tuck into the Indian selection at the party. I mention to my brother-in-law John that I will regret it if I go into labour and throw up again. The delivery room will smell of onion bhajis this time. He laughs.

'You'd best finish them off then.' He passes me the whole box and I willingly oblige.

19/09/2004

I wake up in the early hours with the urge to go to the toilet. I notice the familiar sign of the pink mucus known as the mucus plug. It's the first sign that things are about to start. My stomach is churning so either I am in labour or those onion bhajis are really kicking in. I go downstairs when the familiar 'stop you in your tracks' contraction happens. I drop to my hands and knees and rock until it goes away. My mum is staying with me at the minute as she finally left my dad. I tell her to ring Mick. Again, my trusted brother is to be my taxi to the hospital and Debbie, my labour partner. My mum calls and the contractions are coming thick and fast now. He gets here in double-quick time and rushes me to the hospital in double-quick time. I think he is terrified I am going to give birth in his car. So terrified that when we get to the hospital he runs into reception and forgets to let me out of the car first. He comes back and ushers me in, relieved Daniel is still firmly inside my tummy. Although not for long it seems as I feel a rush of water down my legs whilst stood in the reception. They put me in a wheelchair and take me into a labour suite. The midwife examines me and asks if I am having an epidural. Oh yes, I'm not going to wait this time.

'Well, you might be too late. You are eight and a half centimetres dilated. We probably won't have time.'

'I will make him wait.' The midwife is amused.

'It's not really going to be up to you, but we will give it a go.' They manage to get the epidural in, but it doesn't seem to work much. Daniel is not hanging around and I can feel him coming. Strangely enough though, whilst it's painful it makes it easier for me to push because I push and don't stop until I feel his head come out. One push and then he is delivered, one more for good luck and job done. Daniel Peter James Fox is born at 10:00 am on 19th September 2004. The midwife doesn't put him on me this time, not like they did with Rebecca, but takes him to the side to clean him. I don't think anything of it, but then it strikes me: he isn't making any sound. I look over and both midwives are around him looking intense and rubbing him with towels.

'Is he OK?' I am in a bit of a panic. Before either of them get to answer, I hear the reassuring little squeal of my baby son, followed by the familiar first cry of a newborn baby.

'There's your answer.' They then bring over my new 9lb 5oz little boy. Bless him, he looks like a grumpy little thing; not the beauty that Rebecca was, but still as perfect to me as he could be.

'Hello, Daniel. Your dad is going to be so disappointed he wasn't here to meet you.' Speaking of Peter, the midwife tells me he has rung the hospital and he is on his way home. My mum must have rung him. Speak of the devil, in she walks, with an excited little girl wanting to know where her brother is. Rebecca jumps up onto the bed next to me where I am cradling Daniel.

'Hello, Daniel. I am your big sister. I have been waiting to see you all my life.' A precious moment: seeing my two beautiful children together for the first time. My mum snaps away. She takes one of all three of us on her phone and sends it to Peter.

'It's my turn now.' She prises Daniel away from Rebecca's arms. I curl up on the bed, cuddling my first born. She has to share me now, but I don't want her to ever feel she is less precious now Daniel is here.

20/09/2004

I am on the ward now. So tired. Daniel is fast asleep in the cot. I am awaiting Peter's arrival. The army were pretty good actually... for them. They let him set off as soon as I went into labour and sorted out his flights. He had to get to Edinburgh and pick up his car and drive home. The hospital agreed to bend the rules due to

him being in the services and said he would
be able to come to the ward when he gets
here. I am so tired though I start to drop off
and dream about him. In my dream he is
there in the room stood at the end of my
bed. But of course it's not a dream, I am
half-awake and he really is here.

'Hi, you, come and meet your son.' He
walks over slowly; he looks scared. He looks
at Daniel.

'Can I hold him?'

'Of course, he's yours.' He picks him up
and lifts him towards the ceiling. Peter is so
tall I fear he will touch the roof.

'Hi, son.' He brings him down into his arms,
planting a kiss on his head. He then
reaches over to me, lifts my chin and kisses
me. 'Thank you.'

Peter stays for an hour just holding Daniel;
he doesn't want to put him down, but he is
so tired he keeps dropping off, so I tell him
to go and get some sleep and come back for
us in the morning.

I hear my husband's and daughter's voices
before I see them. 'I'm holding him first...
no, I am... no, me first... no, Daddy, me
first.' I hear the mutual torment of their
voices. Peter ribbing Rebecca, but Rebecca
getting quite frustrated if she doesn't get to

hold him first. She sees me on the ward and comes running over.

'Mummy, Mummy, we have come to take Daniel home.'

'What about me?' She hasn't thought about that.

'You can come too.'

'OK. Thank you.' She jumps on the bed and promptly gets her way and is able to hold him first. Peter sits at the top of the bed with me, putting a protective arm around me. The doctor comes round and gives us the all clear and off all four of us go to start the rest of our lives together as a complete, devoted and happy family. Nothing is going to tear this family apart.

Chapter 6 – Afghanistan

29/09/2006

Our fifth wedding anniversary. My mum is having the kids and Peter is whisking me off to London for the night. He promises me a meal and a show, but doesn't tell me which. He has booked us into a 5-star hotel in the centre of London. It's a bit surreal as I lived in London for three years when I was seventeen and have never been back since. I recognise some bits, but not everything, so it is still exciting to be in the capital. We enjoy a lovely slap up meal at the hotel and off we go to our show; I still don't know which one it is. We are in the theatrical heartland of London and pass many well-known shows, *Les Miserables*, *Cats*, etc. As we round a corner Peter stops and points down the street.

'We're here.' I look down the street and see the famous mask of the *Phantom of the Opera* staring back at me.

'How did you know?'

'Your mum. She said you fell in love with the show even though you have never seen it; that you always said one day you would come to London and see it. So here we are.' He was so right. I dreamed of coming to London to see the *Phantom* as a child.

'I love it.' I fling my arms around him. 'I love you so much.'

'I love you too. Let's go.' We head towards the theatre and enjoy the most wonderful night. My wonderful husband and the romance of the *Phantom of the Opera* make for an exceptional night and a fabulous fifth wedding anniversary.

14/07/2007

Peter rings from Catterick. He has just started a two-year posting there. It will make such a difference as he is only an hour away and we should be able to see more of him. I won't worry as much about the long-distance driving now. He is part of the training team, training new recruits. He seems in his element and is really excelling. He is getting excellent reports and should be on course for promotion to sergeant when he returns to Edinburgh. I don't want to think too far ahead though as when he returns to the regiment he will then begin pre-deployment training for Afghanistan. This will be his first tour. Apart from the six weeks in Iraq and Sierra Leone, we have managed to avoid any serious deployments like this. I will worry about it enough when the time comes, so I put it out of my mind for now.

01/07/2009

How time passes when you are having fun. The two years at Catterick have passed far too quickly. Peter has been home a lot more than normal due to the distance and we have enjoyed quantity as well as quality of time together. We have purposely made the most of it as Peter deploys to Afghanistan on 10th October. Unbelievably it will be his thirtieth birthday then as well. Where has my spotty twelve year old gone? Actually, he has turned into a handsome, devoted and loving husband and father; I am so lucky. We had some photos taken of us today in a photographic studio. We want them done in plenty of time for him to take them with him for the six months he will be on tour so he can keep us close. Six months; I can't imagine being apart from him for that long. It's difficult to push it to the back of my mind now that it's so close.

07/10/2009

It's three days before Peter deploys and I have arranged a surprise party for him at the local dog track. All our family and friends are there waiting for the guest of honour. We walk into the restaurant to cheers from everyone. Rebecca and Daniel did so well to keep it secret. Peter seems shocked but happy. We enjoy the night and have sponsored a race on his behalf. When the DJ announces that we have sponsored the race and are celebrating before he deploys to Afghanistan there are rapturous cheers and applause around the track and in the bars. Peter presents the trophy to the winner and takes an age to get back to us as he is stopped several times on the way by strangers wanting to shake his hand or pat him on the back. It seems we are not the only ones who are proud of him. The night is a great success and Peter takes me to the side and thanks me for arranging it. That night at home he tells me he loves me and the kids so much and that if anything happens to him whilst he is away, he will have lived a happy life and that I should remember how much he loved us. I tell him not to be daft, to keep his head down over there and to come back to us in one piece.

09/10/2009

Peter, Rebecca, Daniel and I are on the platform at Sheffield Train Station. The train to Edinburgh is due any moment. These may be our last moments together. You try not to think about it, but you also don't want to miss saying the things you would if you knew these were your last moments. The train pulls in and Rebecca throws herself into Peter's arms; she is sobbing and clinging to him, not wanting to let him go. I have to pull her off; her face is a crumpled mess of pain and fear. Daniel, I think, is not fully aware of where his daddy is off to, but cries as well, as he thinks he has to if his sister is. Peter hugs him and tells him he is the man of the house and needs to take care of Mummy and Rebecca. The whistle blows signalling the last call for the train; Peter takes me in his arms, lifts my chin and kisses me. I can't stop the tears and neither can he.

'I love you. Whatever happens, remember I always loved you. Since the moment I saw you.'

'OK. I love you too. Keep your head down and come back to us in one piece.' I manage just about to get the words out. He climbs on the train and puts his kit down. He turns around and Rebecca jumps on the train for one last hug; she is clearly going to struggle with this. She is seven now and fully understands where he is going. She is clearly terrified for him. Again I have to pull my sobbing child away from the most important man in her life. A man she adores, her hero, our hero; my life has revolved around him for the last nine years. The doors shut, the whistle blows and the train pulls away. We watch until the train is out of sight. With tears streaming and an emptiness inside, I wrap my arms around my two children and we leave the platform. I can see that people around us realise what is happening and they are clearly affected by the emotions they have just witnessed. They try not to catch my eye, but if they do, they smile in comfort and appreciation. We make our way home, not knowing what tomorrow will bring. We will have to take it one day at a time and hope he is lucky enough to come back.

31/12/2009

Three months since Peter left and he is due back on R&R. His tour is turning out to be the worst one ever. Many young lads have been killed. Afghanistan has never been far from my mind and whilst you try to put it out of your thoughts, for your own sanity, you still fear every unexpected, unknown phone call or knock on the door; families get text messages informing us that someone from the battalion has been killed prior to it being released to the press. Sadly, receiving the text is double-edged as someone has died, but the fact that you have the text means it's not your husband. The texts during this tour have been coming thick and fast.

We are at the station again, waiting his arrival. Rebecca is so excited. She has sent him an e-bluey every day without fail, even if it was just to say hello. When he calls, he tells us how all the lads tell him he must be well loved with all the parcels and letters he receives. He gets more than everyone else. His R&R is just for two weeks and then sadly he will have to return. We have a week's holiday booked so we can spend some quality time together.

'It's here,' Rebecca squeals. She is right; the train is pulling in. We watch intensively to

see if we can spot him. Carriage after
carriage goes past. I can see the camel
colouring of the desert uniforms, but can't
pinpoint him. This is a popular train for
lads returning home. The train pulls to a
halt and the doors swing open; one or two
army lads get off mixed with the regular
civvies, but we still can't see him. We look
down the platform further and there he is.
The 6ft 4 hero in full kit with the biggest
burgen on his back I have ever seen; he still
has his beret on and is desperately
scouring the station looking for us. Rebecca
sees him, pulls her hand out of mine and
shoots down the platform. Suddenly it
seems like the rest of the people around
know what is about to take place and they
clear a path for her to her daddy. He sees
her and in one quick move flicks his burgen
off his back, his beret off his head, kneels
down and opens his arms awaiting the
arrival of his daughter racing towards him.
From what seems like a million miles away,
Rebecca launches herself at him and he
catches her in his big strong arms. He
stands up with her and they are wrapped in
a father/daughter embrace that no one is
tearing apart. They are still wrapped in
each other when Daniel and I get there. We
stand like outsiders for what seems like an
age. I can see people on the train pointing
and smiling at having just witnessed the
most amazing scene and one they only
generally see on TV. Finally, they manage to
break themselves apart and Peter picks up
Daniel in his other arm and somehow

manages to wrap both kids in his arms around me so that we are all one in a precious and happy bundle. We finally manage to stop our tears of joy and start to leave the station to make our way home. We only have two weeks and we need to make the most of it.

We make our way to my brother's for a New Year's Eve party and a celebration of Peter returning. You could tell all night he wasn't really with us, but it's understandable bearing in mind where he had just come from. He didn't talk too much about what had been happening over there, but did tell us all one harrowing incident.

'A four or five-year-old boy, around Daniel's age, was dropped off at the camp gates by a truck. The truck drove out of sight, but we could hear the "chatter" on the radio. As the boy walked towards the camp he was ordered to stop and lift up his top. He did so and revealed a suicide pack strapped to his body. I called for the bomb disposal guys to go out, but they didn't have time. We heard the people in the truck give the instruction to detonate the bomb. The boy was ripped apart in front of my eyes.'

We all fell silent. Speechless. What could we say? What awful things must these lads endure? I have never felt so proud of Peter as I did at that moment. To witness a horror like that and to still be standing is testament to the hero he is. We carry on

with the party and look forward to our week
away in a few days.

02/01/2010

Finally, we make it to Center Parcs. It's only
an hour and a bit away from where we live,
but it has been snowing heavily so it's
taken us over two hours. The snow is
coming thick and fast now so we park up as
close to our cabin as possible and get our
luggage in so we can relax. It's a lovely
scene actually; logs on the fire with snow-
covered trees outside the window. Like an
Aspen ski retreat rather than a cabin in a
holiday park in Nottingham.

'I am glad it's like this. It's so far removed
from Afghanistan that you should be able to
forget about it for the week.' He smiles and
nods, but I know he will struggle to do that
knowing that in two weeks' time he will be
back on patrol in Sangin. We dump our
bags and head off out to have a look around
and get something to eat. As it's only just
past Christmas the decorations and lights
are still up, which adds to the beauty of the
place. The weather has had an effect on
some of the activities, but I don't mind so
long as I have my darling husband safe
here with me and the kids, that's all that
matters. We have a lovely meal in the pub
bar on site and head for the club. The kids
have a great time and we head back,
trudging through the thick snow, to our
cabin. Logs are put on the fire and we all

curl up together on the settee with a hot drink before we make our way to our beds. Peter is so tired that he is the first to suggest we get off to bed. He puts the kids to bed and falls asleep as soon as his head hits the pillow. As I am not the best sleeper in the world, I lie there for a while, watching my hero of a husband. I stroke his hair and face. I am so glad he is back with us in one piece, even if it's just for a short while. His leg twitches under the covers and he mumbles something, but I can't make it out. Tired now myself, I switch the light off, ready to go to sleep. As the light goes off Peter sits bolt upright in bed.

'GET THE FUCK AWAY FROM HER,' he shouts. I reach for the light and switch it back on.

'What's up?' Peter is staring at the end of the bed.

'Sorry. I had a bad dream that Taliban were in the room pulling at my leg and pointing at you, saying they were going to take you; showing me how they were going to slit your throat.'

'It's just a dream. There is no one there.' He looks around the room wide-eyed as if he is following someone. As his eyes reach my side he wraps his arms around me and pulls me to his side of the bed.

'I know. Just leave the light on and let's go back to sleep.' I think nothing more of it and eventually fall asleep in his arms.

09/01/2010

All packed up now and ready to go back home. It's been a nice week just being together as a family. Peter had no more bad dreams and we made the most of things even though the snow meant that apart from the pool nothing much was open, but we had each other. We head off back home to spend our last few days together before he returns to Afghanistan. Another sad goodbye to get through. I try to tell myself that we are halfway there now and the time would pass, but three months is a long time when you spend it playing Russian roulette with your feet, as Peter would tell me.

'Every step you take, you don't know if it's your last.' My poor baby. I know he is scared. He would never say it though. He will go back and do his duty. How amazing and brave. It's no wonder me, Rebecca and Daniel love and adore him so much.

13/01/2010

Here we are again at the station saying our goodbyes. It is no easier than the first time. The train pulls in and I once again have to pull my devastated daughter away from the man she loves. She promises him she will continue to write every day.

'You'd better, Princess. I look forward to your letters every day.' He shakes hands with Daniel and gives him a cuddle. 'Don't forget, you're the man of the house now.' He reaches for me and gives me a kiss and a cuddle. He doesn't tell me the things he did before. I sense this time he is worried, as he knows now what he is returning to. He is on the train and it pulls away. We wave until we can see him no more and off we go back home without him.

14/02/2010

We settle back into our routine at home and try to push Peter to the back of our minds. He isn't able to ring as much now, as things are not great in Sangin. Many more lads have been killed, including one of Peter's good friends. He was gutted; said they are told to put it behind them and get on with the job. He rang a week or so ago and told me there had been an explosion near them. Thank fully no one was killed, but he received a few minor shrapnel wounds. He brushed it off though as nothing. I hadn't heard from him for a week when he rang. He was very subdued.

'I can't talk long. I lost one of my men today. We were on patrol. Our lead man, Green, asked me which way to go. I told him to go through the hole in the wall. I watched as he turned and went through. In a split second there was an explosion. He had stepped on an IED and was killed.

When the dust settled I had to pick up the body parts and bring them back to camp. He is the first man I have lost. It's my fault.'

'Don't be daft. It's not your fault. It's whoever laid the IED's fault.'

'It's not; it's mine. I gave the order. I have to go. We are out on patrol again in a minute.' He put the phone down before I could say goodbye. How awful for him. I know that lads are getting blown up regularly, but you can never imagine what it's like. He actually witnessed it. I try not to think of the fact that it could have been him. He must have been so close. What if he had been the lead man? I have to push it out of my mind otherwise I will drive myself insane.

16/03/2010

The phone rings in the middle of the night. This can only be Peter ringing at this time. I don't mind though. At least he's ringing. Every phone call brings a sigh of relief as you know at least that they are still alive.

'It's me.' He's shouting in a panic. 'They're moving me. Something has happened. I am being accused of firing indiscriminately.'

'Did you?'

'No. I fired at insurgents. I killed them. No one else saw them, only me. They couldn't find them afterwards. They say I caused confusion. The lads are refusing to work with me. They said I've seen too much action. I need to go somewhere quieter for my own benefit.' I tell him to calm down, but he carries on. 'I will get booted out of the army for this.' I again tell him to calm down. If they are moving him to a quieter place, if one exists over there, then that can only be a good thing.

'I suppose so.' He seems to calm down and we have a chat for a while about the kids and then his credit runs out and I go back to sleep.

27/03/2010

It's finally here: the day Peter comes home. We have travelled up to Edinburgh. We are in the gym on camp with other families waiting for their return. There are not as many families as you see on TV, but some have already returned and more are still to come. Only one flight today. He does seem to have had a quieter time now in Kajaki when he was moved from Sangin. He told me he had some interviews with the mental health nurse. It was just routine; something they do for anyone who has seen what he has seen. But he is fine. Nothing to worry about. The plane is delayed and we have a little longer to wait. Rebecca and Daniel are getting a bit bored of waiting. The other kids in the hall are smaller than them and there is a bouncy castle provided that they are enjoying. We sit on our own as we don't know anyone. All the other wives are clearly from camp. They sit huddled and gossiping away. They flick me the odd glance now and again as if I am intruding and should not be there. Finally, the sergeant tells us the coach has pulled up and they will be here in a second. They then start to come in one by one. As the wives and children see them they run to them in lovely scenes of families being reunited; their embraces unbroken as the next and the next returning hero comes through the doors into their loved ones' arms. Then in walks Peter. Rebecca and Daniel run over to him. He looks like he sees them, but can't have done as he deviates from the route they were taking towards him and goes over to the sergeant to shake his hand and talk to him. The kids stop in their tracks and stand waiting for him. He shakes the sergeant's hand again and then turns towards them. They run to him and he lifts them into his arms. That's the scene I was waiting to see. I realise I am the only one stood on my own. Everyone else is embracing. I don't know why, but he looks different. I can't put my finger on it. Whatever it is, it stops me running over and throwing myself into his arms. But then he looks up at me and smiles and I see my soul mate and the love of my life back in one piece. I run over and throw my arms around him. We kiss and hold each other. All four of us. When we come apart people have started to leave. We help him carry his kit to the car. As we leave the sergeant catches his eye.

'Let me know what happens, Peter.'

'I will.' I look at him enquiring. 'It's nothing. Let's get out of here.'

28/03/2010

We arrive back in Sheffield. Little does Peter know, I have arranged a homecoming party for him. I insist on driving back so that I can ensure we don't get home before all our guests have arrived. As we near the house, I notice his dad's car a few cars in front of us. Typical, can't even be bothered to be on time for his own son's homecoming. I make excuses that we need petrol to give them time to get to the house. After getting petrol we head off home. We pull round the corner and you can see the house with all the bunting and flags outside. Everyone is outside cheering and clapping as we pull up. My brother shakes and pops open a bottle of champagne and sprays it all over Peter. Peter shakes everyone's hand and we all go inside and have a wonderful homecoming party for him. Everyone wants to talk to him so I don't get much of a look in, but that's OK, it's his party. He's the hero after all.

06/05/2010

Rebecca, Daniel, my mum, our friends Gary and Kealley, and I are all stood on the streets of Edinburgh. It's the regiment's homecoming parade today. We all travelled up from Sheffield yesterday. It's freezing cold, but we don't care. Our pride will keep us warm. We position ourselves on the corner so that we have a clear view of them coming over the hill. We slowly hear the sound of the bugles and the military music. The regimental band comes first. Then they pass in the individual companies; A first, then B, then C – Peter's company. He has forewarned me where he will stand: right at the back on the right-hand side. The hill is steep enough that I can see him from the distance. I watch him all the way down, whooping and cheering. As he gets closer, Rebecca and Daniel start shouting.

'We love you, Daddy.' I can see Peter smile. They whip off their jackets to show their T-shirts with his picture on one side and 'My Daddy's a Hero' on the other together with his picture. He gets closer and as he passes the kids shout again. 'Love you, Daddy.' Again he smiles, but doesn't turn and carries on marching down the hill and out of sight. What a proud moment and the day is not over yet; we are heading up to camp for a family day. They have a funfair, BBQ and lots of other entertainment on and the medals parade will take place.

After the medals parade, we all enjoy the party. The lads have found their families and you see many proud wives, mums, dads, children, friends, etc. hanging onto their heroic loved ones for dear life. Peter is not here yet. He rang and said he won't be long, just had something to do. It's a lovely warm day so we tuck into the massive spread that is on for the BBQ. After another hour Peter gets here. I am a bit annoyed, not with him, but with the army for making him work when his family is here. I feel like we have missed out on some precious time. Anyway, he is here now and we enjoy the rest of the day. Peter wanders off now and again to say goodbye to friends, but eventually we call it a day and head off back to the hotel and the train journey home tomorrow. Then we have him to ourselves for three weeks whilst he is on leave.

Chapter 7 – It wasn't me

09/05/2010

The excitement of the last few days has worn off and we are at home just relaxing together. Peter is quite subdued, but this is to be expected. It's his first chance to relax since he got back from Afghanistan. The regiment sends all families a booklet explaining all the finer details of deployment pre-, during and post-op. It did say that post-operations there would be a period of adjustment for the men where they need to readjust to normal family life. He is laid on the settee when the kids jump on him asking him to come out to play. In one quick move he jumps up, sending them both flying onto the floor. They both scramble to their feet crying, more in shock than them being hurt. Peter sits back down and says nothing.

'Hey. What's that all about?'

'I don't want them jumping on me.'

'They're excited to have you home. They just want to spend some time with you.'

'I know. I will play with them in a bit.' He apologises to them both. They accept his apology and trudge off outside anyway to play with their friends. I sit next to him and ask if there is something wrong. He says 'no', but I can tell there is. I push him to tell me. Eventually he tells me that since he got back he has been told he would be disciplined for three different instances in Afghanistan. He says it's all down to one of the officers, who doesn't like him, making up lies and turning all the lads against him. He says it's his word against an officer's and he has no chance of proving his innocence. He has to write a statement on what happened and hand it in to the CO when he gets back. I grab my laptop and tell him to start talking and I will type the statement up. I don't want this hanging over him the whole three weeks and ruining our time together. He gives me a kiss and seems relieved. Then he starts telling me his version of events.

SANGIN

'I was on patrol with my Company. We had been patrolling for over an hour and came upon a compound. We surrounded the perimeter of the compound. Lead man Green radioed through to me asking which way I wanted him to go. I gave the order to go through the gap in the perimeter wall and we would follow through from there. I could see Green. He gave me the thumbs up as well as OK-ing my instruction over the radio. I watched as he turned and proceeded to move towards the gap in the wall. On his second step forward there was an explosion. I was knocked off my feet and hit the ground. Suddenly, there was gunfire from in front of us. The lads panicked and

fired back. I called to them to cease fire. I
stood up and walked over to where Green
had been. Bits of his body were spread out
over about fifty metres. I identified his body
armour flicked up over his head. I
approached and pulled his armour back.
Green's head was missing from the bit of
his torso that was left with only his jaw line
and bottom teeth in place. I placed the
armour back so the men would not see this.
I radioed one KIA back to camp and the
relevant extraction process was put in to
place. As we waited for the stretchers, we
picked up as many body parts as we could.
Once the sergeant arrived and extracted the
body back to camp we all returned.'

SANGIN

'I was part of the team guarding the guys
clearing trees from the Green Zone. There
was an explosion to the right and I saw two
insurgents behind where the explosion was.
I opened fire and killed them. There was
then rapid fire from the distance and we all
took cover and I gave the order to return
fire. After about twenty minutes the firing
stopped. As we looked through our
binoculars we could see three motorbikes
coming down the dirt road towards us.
There were three men and one woman. The
woman was bleeding from a wound to the
neck. The interpreter said they claimed we
had shot her. I called for a medic and the
woman was treated. The others were taken

away for questioning and I and my team returned to camp.'

KAJAKI

'We were on a routine patrol. As we walked up the hill I noticed movement in the distance. I called for an RPG. We walked forward to get in a better position with the lead man Smith as vallon man. As we walked I dropped the RPG and it rolled a little down the slope. I shouted to Smith to keep walking. I walked down the slope and as I got to the RPG I heard an explosion above me and I was showered with dust and debris. When the smoke had cleared I climbed back up the slope and saw a crater ahead of me. I could see Smith face down in the crater. I approached him and realised he was dead. I radioed through one KIA and called for a stretcher and for some of the lads to help me pick up the body. Four of us picked him up and his whole body crumbled in our hands. It felt like a man-size bean bag as all the bones in his body had been shattered into a thousand pieces. We managed to get him onto the stretcher, covered him up and took him back to camp.'

I finish typing the statements and then close down the computer.

'Now that's done you can enjoy the rest of your leave. Get out and play with the kids.'

It was no wonder he was a bit on edge with all this on his mind.

31/05/2010

Back to routine again. Peter kissed me goodbye as he left for the long drive back to Edinburgh. He had managed to put things out of his mind and enjoyed himself with the kids. In fact he enjoyed himself too much. He took the kids to McDonald's every day for something to eat whilst I was at work. They concocted a story between them that the kids didn't have anything to eat. I could see through it though. I knew they were just trying to stop their dad getting into trouble for feeding them junk every day. Rebecca insisted they didn't have anything, even putting on a sad face. Daniel joined in too, saying they even had to pinch a chip when he went to the toilet. I knew nothing had gone from the fridge and I saw the look Peter gave them to not grass him up. I wasn't bothered though. Life's too short. Why not let them eat crap for a week with their hero of a dad after the six months they had been without him?

01/06/2010

I am at work when Peter rings.

'Hello, my dear. How's things?'

'Kathryn, I am going to get booted from the army.' The panic was back in his voice like it was in Afghanistan.

'What? Why? Did you hand in your statement?' Apparently he had.

'Yes. They said they are a load of crap and I am going to be charged. I have been moved out of my unit and on to crappy duties. No one will talk to me. I don't know what is going on. I don't know what this is all about. No one will tell me.'

'They can't do that. They will have procedures to follow. I will look into things.'

15/06/2010

I have spent the last two weeks researching and reading up on MOD disciplinary procedures. It's very clear they have not followed protocol. I complete a Subject Access Request for Peter to hand in to get access to his files to see what had been said. Apparently the adjutant tore it up in front of his face and said he was getting nothing. I decide to write to our MP to see if she could help. In the meantime, Peter has become very depressed and has started to be agitated with me and the kids; but I understand. Who would not be stressed with this hanging over them?

03/07/2010

Saturday morning and I have had a lie in. I leave Peter asleep. He was tired after the long drive. He had gone straight to bed last night when he got home. Snapped again at the kids. They wanted him to play with them, but he was too tired. The post has already arrived. I notice an official-looking letter. It is from my MP. She has had a response from the MOD. In a nutshell they agree correct procedures have not been followed. The clerk had forged Peter's signature on official documents as if he had seen them. The disciplinary would be redone from scratch. I take it up to Peter. He reads it.

'It means nothing. I will still get kicked out. Everyone is out to get me. Making up lies. I can't trust anyone.'

'It will be OK.' I try to reassure him, but nothing I say changes his mood.

Later that day, Peter is laid on the settee when Daniel comes in and sits next to him.

'Dad, can you come outside and play football?'

'No. I'm tired.'

'Please, Daddy. If you don't, I will throw the ball at you.' Peter sits up, grabs the ball from him with one hand and hits him in the stomach with the other.

'You do, you little bastard, and I will slit your throat.' Daniel screams in pain.

'Dad! You don't have to hit me that hard.' He bursts into tears and runs to me.

'What the hell do you think you are doing?' I have never seen him hit him before.

'Why can't he leave me alone? Why can't everyone leave me alone?'

'He wants to play with his dad, like he used to. Is that too much to ask?'

'I don't want to play with him or Rebecca. I can't do this.'

He storms upstairs. I send the kids outside and follow him up. We have a blazing row, which culminates in me telling him to go back to camp as I don't want him here in this mood. He has ruined the weekend.

07/07/2010

I haven't heard from Peter for a few days and I am still mad enough to not ring him either. Finally, he rings.

'I'm so sorry, babe. I should never have spoken to you or the kids like that. I love you more than anything. You are the only one who is there for me. There is still all this shit going off at work. I don't know what to do. I shouldn't take it out on you and the kids. Please don't leave me.'

'I wouldn't.'

'You are. You are going to leave me. You should. I don't deserve you.'

'I'm not. I will stand by you, whatever. We will get through this. I promise. If you get kicked out, you will still have me and the kids; but it won't come to that,' I reassure him.

'OK. I feel a bit better now. You are still coming to the Summer Ball with me, aren't you?'

'Try and stop me,' I tell him. Any excuse to get my ball gown out.

18/07/2010

The day of the Summer Ball. I have travelled up from Sheffield to Edinburgh and Peter has picked me up from the station. He takes me to the hotel I have booked, which is just round the corner from the venue. He has to nip back to work and will be back later. I hang up my lovely ball gown. I have lost weight and this is the first time I will wear it. It's a designer one I bought in the sale a year ago. Typical dieter, I bought it saying I would slim into it. Fortunately, on this occasion, I have and it looks lovely on. I relax in the room for a while watching TV before I start to get ready. The ball starts at 18:30 so there is plenty of time.

I think in my excitement I may have got ready too soon. I am an hour early. All dressed up in my lovely ball gown with nowhere to go. I feel like Cinderella waiting for Prince Charming to arrive. Peter has still not got back yet. He rang and said he was setting off an hour ago. If he doesn't get here soon, he won't have time to get changed. Finally, he gets here with half an hour to spare. I don't get any explanation other than he had stuff to do at work. I don't question any further as I don't want to delay him anymore. He gets ready in double-quick time and off we go to the ball. He comments on how beautiful I look and I return the compliment on how handsome he is. It's only a two-minute walk to the hotel where the ball is being held. As we get closer we can see the coach that has brought other lads and their wives from camp. Many are stood outside having a cigarette. We enter the doors and take advantage of the free glass of champagne on offer. We take our place at the bar, just the two of us. Now and again someone will say hello to Peter, but predominantly we are on our own; that is a disadvantage of not living on camp as I don't know anyone to talk to and Peter has to stick by my side. The call comes for everyone to go through to the hall for the meal. We walk in and the tables are filling up. Groups of friends sit together. Again another disadvantage for me not knowing anyone. We find some spare seats on a table and sit down. Peter knows the people vaguely so is able to make pleasantries. The meal is lovely and I feel suitably stuffed. We go back to the bar whilst the tables are cleared away for the disco. I am sat at the bar again with Peter when I hear a vaguely familiar voice behind.

'Hi, Mrs Fox.' I spin round and recognise the face, a few years older now, but I remember; it's Clarky, the third of the three musketeers from Cyprus.

'Hello.' I get up and give him a hug and a kiss. It appears he rejoined a few years ago as he missed the military life and couldn't settle as a civilian. He sits next to me and we start to chat. We catch up on old times and what we have been up to. We discuss Jacko and the kids, his and mine. The conversation then turns to Peter.

'He is not himself, is he? He's not the bloke I knew back then. He has no fight in him. He doesn't talk to anyone. He's distant. He's just not right.' I immediately jump on the defensive. It is understandable with what was going on at work; Clarky should know that. He knows that Peter is green through and through and it's a stab in the back to be accused of not doing his job right. Clarky wouldn't have it. 'Kathryn, he's not right.' With that, he kisses me on the cheek and off he goes. Talking to Clarky has given Peter a chance to disappear. I can't see where he is, but he finally comes back.

'You OK?' I nod. I don't tell him what Clarky said. It's nonsense as far as I am concerned. The night draws to an end and we return to our hotel. We spend the next day together and I return home the following day, not giving Clarky's comments a second thought.

18/08/2010

Things have eased off a bit now at work whilst the investigation is going on. Peter is still very withdrawn though. We are on our way to the airport for a two-week holiday to Greece. Peter doesn't seem to have much patience with the kids, but they seem to have got used to it; they don't bother him with asking to play with them anymore. But we are on holiday now; a million miles away from the crap back home.

02/09/2010

Back from holiday. Had a lovely time. Peter would get up even before I woke to put towels down on the beds for us. Hotel was lovely and food was great. All inclusive. Only problem was we were on the flight path so we would get woken early with planes flying in. I would wake up with a scare with the noise.

06/09/2010

Back to routine after the holiday. Peter went back to camp this morning and hasn't rung me yet, so I ring him. He doesn't answer. Then he rings me straight back.

'What do YOU want?'

'Nothing. Just ringing. Where were you?'

'Are you fucking spying on me? I am not at your beck and call. FUCK OFF, CUNT.'

'I beg your pardon?' I'm stunned.

'Not you. Someone has just come in my room.'

'Don't you have a lock on your door?'

'Yes, but they still come in.'

'Get the lock fixed then.'

'It's not broken.'

He then launches into a tirade of crude and explicit sexual acts he wants to do to me this weekend. He seems unembarrassed to say it in front of the people in his room.

'You can't say that in front of people.'

'They've gone.' *Short visit*, I think. I didn't even hear their voices. He continues with his sexual tirade. I finish the conversation as quickly as I can and put the phone down. That was so weird. He has never spoken to me so crudely, forcefully and with no emotion. It makes me feel a little sick to my stomach. The disciplinary must be stressing him out. That kind of language is not him.

15/12/2010

These last few months have been horrendous. The glimpses of the old Peter are getting less and less. His mood swings have got worse. He is snappy with me and the kids all the time. He says nasty stuff to them during the day and then denies saying it when I challenge him. When I ring him, if he answers, he seems OK at first and then shouts at me to leave him alone. I can't say or do anything right. He doesn't touch me at night when he gets back and then all but rolls on and off in the morning. Sex, when it happens, seems forceful and unemotional, which makes me inclined not to participate, which then causes arguments. I feel sometimes that he can't bear to look at me. He jumps down my throat at the smallest of things and we are constantly arguing. I am scared the arguments will escalate and get physical. He spends no time with the kids at weekends and they are beginning to dread him coming home and ask not to be left alone with him or go with him in his car. I understand he is stressed because of this black cloud hanging over him, but he seems and sounds utterly depressed and totally obsessed with losing his job. He's paranoid that everyone hates him at work and is back-stabbing him; says me and the kids treat him like shit. He has started coming home later than normal and going back earlier with the oddest of excuses. But I am beginning to worry there is someone else. When I suggest this he gets angry that I could even think such a thing. He twists this then and accuses me of cheating on him. There isn't anything I can do now in respect of the disciplinary as they are following the correct procedures so we just have to wait for the outcome, but his behaviour is really starting to grind me and the kids down. I am so miserable, so sad. I feel lost as I have no idea how things got like this. I can't make sense of it and don't know how to put this right. It wasn't meant to be like this. I put on a brave face to everyone. Family and friends think everything is fine. The stress of it all has caused me to lose more weight. People comment how great I look, but I am dying inside – not a diet I would recommend.

16/12/2010

My mobile rings at work. It's Peter. I ignore it. I really can't do with another argument. It has started to affect my work. I hate my job. My employers are having a restructure and have offered voluntary redundancies. I seriously wish I could take up the offer.

Requests have to be in by the end of March. It's out of the question though, especially as I am beginning to feel like me and Peter need to separate and I will become a single mum with a mortgage to pay. I need my job. But it's Christmas and I want us to have a good one. We have invited Peter's nan up for Christmas day as well; after all, last year he was in Afghanistan at this time. My phone beeps. Peter has text.

'Babe, please pick up the phone. I need to talk to you. I have good news.' He rings again and I answer.

'What?' I keep my guard up.

'Babe, it's all over. It's been thrown out. I have nothing to answer for. I was telling the truth all along and all the others were lying. I have been given the equivalent of a slap on the wrist. The CO said he has to give me this. I can't believe it's all finally over. I am so sorry, babe. I know I have been horrible these last few months. I will make it up to you and the kids when I am home on leave. I love you. Thank you for believing in me and sticking by me. You and the kids mean everything to me.'

So he's back again; the Peter I know. Maybe this is going to be OK. It must have been awful for him, after all he is green through and through and would have been lost had he been kicked out. Being in the army is all he has ever wanted. I dreaded how depressed he would have got had he been kicked out.

'I'm glad.' I tell him we have been invited out on the 23rd with our friends from Rebecca's school.

'Great. We can celebrate all this shit being over.' We finish our conversation and go back to our jobs. I feel like a weight has been lifted. He must feel even better having had to deal with it every day. Thoughts of separating are now dismissed from my mind. How could I have been so selfish to have even contemplated leaving him? They are replaced with looking forward to him coming home this weekend for his Christmas leave and finally getting on with our lives.

23/12/2010

We are on our way to the pub to meet our friends. My mum is babysitting at home. We have had a lovely few days since Peter came home now the crap of this last year is finally over. I feel like I have my Peter back. I realise he was lost for a while and had been replaced by a cold, unfeeling, distant stranger. Things are even back to normal in the bedroom. I have been looking forward to tonight. Peter doesn't drink and normally drives, but wanted to let his hair down and enjoy himself. We meet Nick and Diane in the pub and start to enjoy our night. We are back to normal, holding hands, kissing and cuddling. 'Get a room,' Nick and Diane comment. The drinks are flowing and all our troubles are forgotten. There are lots of young girls out in skimpy Santa Claus outfits. Peter doesn't look at them and only has eyes for me. It's amazing. I feel like he is acting again how he did when we first met. After two kids though and nearly ten years of marriage, I am a bit down on the way I look, despite losing so much weight. As Peter is a lot younger than me, I keep commenting on the young girls in the skimpy Santa outfits.

'Not a patch on you, Kathryn.' A reassuring comment from Nick.

'Thanks.' I joke with Peter, 'Why aren't you saying that?' He just laughs. Maybe he doesn't think he has to. Of course, he doesn't; he is with me and has always shown his undying love for me, apart from this last year. We carry on with our lovely night. Last orders have been called and Nick and Peter fetch our last drinks. They take a while to drink and we are all happy and tipsy. The lights come on and we leave after having a fantastic night. Peter flags a cab and we say our goodbyes and wish Nick and Diane a Happy Christmas. We set off. On the way I see yet another young girl in a skimpy Santa outfit.

'Look at her. What would you think if I dressed like that?'

'Well, you wouldn't. They look like slags and it wouldn't suit you. You're too old.' I tell him 'thanks' as I think he's joking, but he carries on.

'Why have you gone on and on about it?'

'I haven't.' I still think he is joking.

'You have done my head in wanting me to say nice things all night. Why should I have to reassure you I love you? You clearly don't love me.'

'Of course I do. Why are you being like this?' I realise now he is not joking.

'No, you don't. I've been told you don't. You have come onto Nick all night. Why don't you fuck off with him if you don't love me? No one loves me.'

'Don't be silly. You're not making sense. Who told you I don't love you?' He is angry now.

'No one you know.' He carries on arguing with me all the way home. I am so embarrassed by the time we get back and I am fuming. I get out of the taxi when we pull up at home. I storm in the house. I am crying now and tell my mum to keep him away from me while I run straight upstairs. Peter comes in and my mum asks what has happened. He tells her nothing and comes upstairs. I am sat on the bed crying. He comes in and grabs my wrists to pull me up.

'Why are you being like this? I love you.' I tell him to leave me alone and I try to pull my wrists out of his grasp. He holds on tighter. 'No. You're not leaving me.'

I tell him to let go of me. He holds my wrists tighter again. It hurts now, so I struggle with all my might to get my wrists from his grasp. I get my right hand free and instinctively slap him. In a split second, everything seems to go black and I feel the right side of my face explode. He's punched me. I am now laid back on the bed. I literally see stars and the pain kicks in. My eyesight in my right eye is blurred. My cheek feels like it's been smashed in two. I can taste the blood running into my mouth from the split in my lip and I can feel it has already swollen. One of my teeth is sharp and feels broken.

'What have you done?' I'm hysterical.

'I didn't touch you.'

'Get away from me.' I run into the bathroom. My eye is bloodshot, swollen and black. My cheek is red and starting to bruise and it hurts like mad. My lip is swollen and split, although the cut does not warrant the amount of blood seeping into my mouth. My tooth is not too bad but painful. I look horrendous. My mum and the kids come upstairs. Rebecca and Daniel cry in horror when they see my face.

'What the hell is going on?'

'She hit me first.'

'Did you?' I tell my mum 'yes', as technically I did hit him first.

'But look at me, mum. I am calling the police. He has broken my cheekbone; I need to go to hospital.'

'Please don't. There is no need, I will go.'

'There is, you're crazy.' I phone the police and ask for an ambulance.

'You have ruined my career, you bitch.' He starts running round the house shouting at me. My poor babies are crying, terrified. 'It's your mum's fault if I get jailed, not mine.' My mum takes them to another room.

He continues to follow me around flipping between profusely apologising and saying he loves me to paranoia saying I have always hated him, my family hate him, I have ruined his career, and says he has been told I have cheated on him. I say it's not true, but he won't believe me and won't say who said it. His behaviour is so irrational and I am so scared. I try to keep out of his way. I seriously fear he is going to hurt me again and do worse damage.

Thankfully, the police arrive and he is handcuffed and taken away. The paramedic looks at my face and suggests we go to hospital for an X-ray. I walk out of the house and get into the paramedic's car as the police car is pulling away. I see the curtains twitching on most of the houses. How embarrassing is this going to be in the morning? But that's not my concern at that minute. The alcohol is wearing off and my face is on fire. I have never felt so much pain.

24/12/2010

I have arrived at the hospital, have seen the Triage Nurse and I am sat alone waiting for the X-ray of my cheek. I have been here for thirty minutes already. There is only me and two others; one drunk asleep on the floor and another young lad slumped in a chair with a bandage round his head. Clearly he has fallen over drunk and hit his head. The shock of tonight's events is kicking in. I am in so much pain, but strangely I feel guilty. This is all my fault. Why did I go on about those girls? Why did I slap him? Why did I call the police? All he wanted was a good night out after a horrible year. What have I done? If the army find out, he will be in so much trouble. He was right: I have ruined his career. I am a terrible wife. He deserves better than this. As I sit, feeling more and more remorseful, the two police officers arrive who arrested him earlier.

'How are you feeling?'

'Embarrassed.'

'You have no need to be.' They are nice, comforting.

They have come to take my statement, but will wait till I have had the X-ray and seen the doctor. It's an hour more before I go in. I spend it talking to them, not about the night's events, but about what a hero Peter is; what a great husband and father he is; how badly the army has treated him; what a bad time he has had this last year, etc. Dutiful army wife mode, defending my man. I finally get called in. The X-ray shows my cheekbone is fine and there should be no lasting damage. My face will be black and blue for a few weeks and Christmas photos won't look good, but other than that and the pain I will mend. The police officers are waiting to take my statement in a little room near reception. I have had time to think. If I miss out the bit about him grabbing my wrists and say I hit him first then he can claim self-defence and it will be my fault. The army cannot criticise him then. So that's what I tell them. They don't judge me, but confirm what I thought. In fact, they say he could file a complaint against me as I hit him first. By now I am so tired I just want to go home to bed. Eventually, after taking photos of my injuries, we are all done and they take me home. My mum and the kids are asleep so I take some pain killers, go to bed and cry myself to sleep.

I have only been asleep a few hours when I hear a whisper.

'Kathryn.' It's my mum. I keep my head hid under the cover.

'Please, mum, I just want to be left alone.' I don't want her to see my face.

'The police are on their way up. They need to talk to you.' Damn. I have to get up. I turn over and my mum gasps. She doesn't say anything, but she is clearly horrified. The hangover has kicked in now; the pounding coming from inside my head now as well as outside. I hurt so much I can't even wash my face to take off last night's make up. I come down as the police officer arrives. He is not one of the nice ones from earlier.

'I won't keep you long, Mrs Fox.' He just needs me to sign a document saying I won't prosecute Peter and he won't me, as I hit him first. I hesitate to sign as my common sense has started to come back and I feel like it is a very bad idea not to make Peter accountable for this. I always said I would never let a man lay a finger on me. I ask the officer what will happen if I decide to prosecute. He tells me the army will have to be called and he will be in a whole load of trouble and will probably get kicked out. He mentions that he is ex-army himself. In fact, he is from Peter's Regiment. He recalls Peter and tells me he is a good lad. He wouldn't have done this had I not hit him first. He talks to me like it's my fault. He makes me feel like a right bitch for putting Peter in this position. My head is banging, my face is hurting and I just want to go back to bed. I sign and off he goes after telling me Peter will be released this morning and asking if I want him to come back to the house. Apparently I can't stop him as it's his house too.

'No.' I don't want him near me. I'm done with him as far as I am concerned.

I have managed to get a few more hours' sleep when the house phone rings and wakes me up. It doesn't ring for long as my mum grabs it quickly. I know she will have been telling everyone what has gone on. She loves a drama, no matter how big or small. I hear her come upstairs.

'Kathryn, it's Peter. Do you want to talk to him?'

'No.'

'Please. He is in a right state.' I agree, if nothing more than to get rid of him. No way am I backing down.

'What?'

'Babe, I know you hate me right now, but please believe me, I am so sorry. It wasn't me. I can't believe what I have done. I can't even remember doing it or what it was all about. All this shit at work has messed my head up. I hate myself and the monster I've become. Please don't leave me. I can't lose you too.'

'What else have you lost?'

'Everything. All this at work.'

'You got cleared. You haven't lost anything.'

'Yes, but I am still being moved. Kicked out of the Regiment. Mud sticks. I have to go on a posting and they never want me back. My career is ruined. I will be on shit duties for the rest of my service.'

'Why didn't you tell me?'

'I was embarrassed. I wanted you and the kids to still be proud of me. But you won't be after this. Please, can I come home? Let me make it up to you over Christmas. I love you and the kids. I can't live without you. Help me get through this.'

Against my better judgement, army wife kicks in again and I relent. I tell him he can come home and we will spend Christmas together for the kids' sake. After that I want time apart to get my head straight and I want him not to touch me. He reluctantly agrees. After an hour he arrives back, gives my mum a lift home and then does as I ask and leaves me alone.

I get up later to find him laughing and playing with the kids on the Wii. Something I have not seen for quite a while now. It's the first time he has seen my face. I think he is too embarrassed to comment on it; just wants to forget about it all. The kids are happy and smiling and they ask me to join in the game. How awful a mum would I be to continue the fight when they seem so happy? So I take my place beside them and join in the fun. Nothing more is mentioned on the events of the night before.

Chapter 8 – The monster

25/12/2010

Christmas Day. I am up early. Not to get the turkey in, but to patch up my face with make up so my black eye, bruised cheek and fat lip don't look so bad when Peter's nan arrives. I can't let her down and tell her not to come. The kids are looking forward to her coming. The kids love her to bits and have even waited to open their presents until she arrives. Plus, she can entertain them whilst I hide in the corner licking my wounds. Peter is doing his best to make up for things; says for me to enjoy the day. He will take care of everything. He does try to be affectionate, but I pull back. Even though I am dying for a kiss and cuddle to make it all go away, any weakness is soon forgotten when the shooting pain in my cheek kicks in. I am not sure that X-ray was correct about my cheekbone not being broken. It bloody feels like it is. Peter put the turkey in before he went to fetch his nan and has just returned. She greets me with a kiss. I must have done a good cover job as she mentions nothing of my swollen face. The hours of crying haven't helped and my other eye is swollen and puffy also. I have put my glasses on to hide as much as I can. Peter brings me a glass of wine. Not sure I should, bearing in mind all the pain killers I have taken. But what the heck, it's Christmas. The pain killers haven't worked anyway; the wine might help. Christmas dinner is quite alright actually, to say Peter and the kids did it all. They seem to have managed to work well as a team. Quite enjoyed themselves. It was nice to see them spending time together again. Like old times. We settle down to the evening's usual crap on TV. So crap that actually we all end up laughing at old Mr Bean programmes. I think the wine is working. The pain has dimmed and I find that I'm enjoying myself. I am sat next to Peter on the settee and I realise he is holding my hand. My head says to pull away, but my heart says not. These moments of affection have been few and far between since he returned from Afghanistan. I enjoy it while I can as he still has to go after Christmas. The night draws to an end and we all reluctantly get off to bed. Margaret is staying the night in Rebecca's room so Peter will have to come back in with me. He swapped with Rebecca the night before as I did not want him near me. I instinctively turn my back on him in bed, but he turns and puts his arm around me and pulls me to his side of the bed. I should pull back, but I don't. It feels like when we were at Center Parcs when he had the bad dream, like he is protecting me. I like the feeling and enjoy it for a minute or two before I drift off to sleep. The wine again, no doubt.

31/12/2010

New Year's Eve. Peter is still here. I have let him stay for the kids' sake as they have been getting along great. He has been making up for lost time. It would break their hearts for me to send him away now. I have told him he can stay till he goes back to camp on the Monday and then I want some time apart; although I said that a few days ago. Today is ten years since we met. He has been so good for the last few days. I am really not sure I can throw away ten years without a fight. I watch him all day. He is the old Peter. The one I fell in love with. I just can't do it. This poor man has endured such a horrific time this past year. Surely I can gift him one mistake. Deep down I know it would hurt far more to let him go than it would to swallow my pride and let him back in. Marriage is about the ups and downs, and until now it has always been up. I can't let my marriage fail at the first hurdle. I decide there and then that I can't let him go. We talk later that night.

'If you ever do anything like this to me again, there will be no more chances.'

'I swear on the kids' lives, I will never hurt you again.' He starts crying. 'You have no idea how bad I feel looking at your broken face, knowing I did that to you. I was so worried you would leave me.' I comfort him.

'It will be OK. I love you too much to let you go.'

04/01/2011

Peter is back in camp. The last few days of his leave were peaceful. I am still a bit cautious and Peter has been treading on eggshells around me. He was great with the kids though. They have enjoyed finally having their dad back. Peter rings.

'Hi, babe, you OK?'

'Yes.' I am sat watching daytime TV. I don't go back to work till the 10th, which is good as hopefully the last of the bruises will have gone by then.

'I have been offered some postings. I can choose, which is good. I can be out of here by the end of January.' He sounds upbeat. 'I had a long chat with my CO. He reckons it will be good for me to move away from the Regiment. A fresh start. I finally feel like things are moving on.'

'Good.'

He tells me he won't be able to ring for a few days and won't be home this weekend as he has to go down to Cambridge to deliver some training and is then on weekend guard.

'OK.' This is no big deal; in fact, it's quite normal. Normal is good.

10/01/2011

Back to work today. I arrive in the office full of beans. All the drama of Christmas is over with.

'Did you have a good one, Kathryn?'

'Yes, really good.' I lied.

'What's wrong with your eye?' *Damn, I thought I had covered up the yellow remnants of my black eye with my make up.*

'I was elbowed in the face at karate.' I leave it at that and scuttle off to my office. Deep down I feel so ashamed for lying, but they wouldn't understand.

That night my brother rings to see if we fancy going on holiday with him, my sister, their partners and kids. Actually, yes, I do. The dates are fine. It's the two weeks after my fortieth birthday, so I know Peter is off on leave then. Will be good for us to have a family holiday together. I'll book it now as a surprise for Peter.

15/01/2011

It's Saturday. Peter is home. He got back late last night. In fact, so late we had already gone to bed so I didn't get a chance to tell him about the holiday. I have let him have a lie in, but me and the kids can't wait any longer and run into the bedroom to wake him up.

'Daddy, Daddy. We're all going on a holiday. Mummy has booked a holiday. We are going with Uncle Michael, Aunty Debz, Uncle John, Aunty Siobhan, Oliver, Dani and Shay.' Peter sits up.

'Oh. What about me, aren't I coming?'

'Of course you are, Daddy.' They know he was kidding them.

'Oh no. Two whole weeks with you two monkeys. What a nightmare.' They burst out laughing and jump on him again. He wraps them both in his arms and tickles and kisses them until they are so worn out that they retreat to their rooms. He turns to me, lifts my chin and plants one of those kisses that have disappeared for over a year now.

'I can't wait. I have good news too. My posting has come through. I leave Edinburgh on 28th January. I think this will be good for me. Good for us. A fresh start.'

I am so pleased. Everything is looking up. He pulls me to him and we lay curled up on the bed together. I feel so at ease I fall asleep in his arms.

11/03/2011

Friday and Peter is home. He has been on his posting for about six weeks now. It has been good for him, but all the driving is taking its toll. He finishes later on this posting than he did in Edinburgh and he has to come home via the M25. It takes much longer to get home and is a far less scenic drive. He has to go back earlier than he used to so as to try and avoid the heavy traffic. This results in us having much less time together at weekends; barely a full day as he is so tired he gets up after me and the kids do. But we make the most of our time together, quality over quantity.

25/03/2011

Another late return for Peter. It is starting to have a negative effect on him. He is so tired and it's causing him to be grumpy and miserable with me and the kids. Action in the bedroom has become rushed and unemotional again due to lack of time, if it happens at all. I raise his attitude with him as I don't want it to get to where it was before; after all, he is happy at work now.

'I know I've not been the best at home. It's due to all the driving. The M25 is a pain. It's not a nice trip. I do it for you, but I wish you and the kids were with me. I wish you were there all the time. Then I wouldn't have to drive. I feel jealous of other blokes whose wives and kids are on camp with them. I know you don't want that, but it is just making me resent the fact that you're not with me.'

It's the first time in ten years me not being on camp with him has been a problem. He is clearly struggling with this. It suddenly strikes me that the answer could be staring me in the face.

'I hate my job. You miss us. We miss you. We finally got back on track and don't want to be apart. Why don't I take up the offer of redundancy and move to camp?' He sits in silence at first.

'But you never wanted to come with me. I can't ask you to do that.'

'You're not asking. It's my decision. I want to do this, to show how much I love you. We've been through so much; I just want to be with you all the time. We have wasted enough time apart. I don't want to waste any more.'

We talk long into the night. It's in the early hours of the morning that we decide that, yes, this is the answer. I will put my redundancy request in on Monday, just in time for the deadline.

15/04/2011

Good news. My redundancy application has been accepted. I will finish work at the end of August. I ring Peter to tell him.

'Oh.'

'Is that all you can say?'

'I don't think it's a good idea.'

'What! Bit late now. I can't take it back. Why is it not a good idea?'

'You will hate it here. You will resent me.'

'I won't. We talked about this.'

'We didn't. You just decided. You always decide. You don't ask me anything. I am fed up of your shit, telling me what to do all the time. I don't want you to come down here.' My heart sinks. Why is he telling me this now? 'I have to go. I will ring you later.'

19/04/2011

Peter didn't ring me later. In fact, he didn't call me back all week. I tried ringing him and texting, but there was no answer. I am out of my mind with worry. I have no idea what is going on. I don't know why he is being like this. Maybe there is someone else and he just doesn't have the guts to tell me. I can't bear to imagine that; that is one step too far. I could not handle that. It would tear me apart. Even thinking it's a possibility makes me want to cry. It's Friday and I don't even know if he is coming home. The kids hope he doesn't. They pretty much give him a wide berth now. They prefer playing with the other dads on the street. Time ticks on and there is still no sign of him. Me and the kids go to bed. I am so confused, so lonely. I'm angry and frustrated. I feel like I am on an emotional rollercoaster, blindfolded. I can't see what's coming next and I can't get off. I am fearful

of the future; fearful of a future without
him and fearful of a future with him. I don't
have an answer for what I want to do to
comfort myself. As I start to drop off I hear
the door go. It must be reaching midnight.
He comes and gets into bed. He puts his
arm around my waist and I push him away.

'Bitch!' I pretend I didn't hear it. My senses
fear an episode like Christmas would kick
in if I react. I lie in bed stone cold silent. I
daren't move. Then I hear him snore. I relax
slightly, knowing he is out for the count.
Either this is madness or I am going mad.

20/04/2011

I wake up and turn over. He is not there,
thankfully. This weekend is no doubt going
to be another miserable one. I hear him
come upstairs. I lie back down and pretend
to be asleep. He comes in and chucks
something at me. It hits me in the eye and I
flinch so I can't pretend I am not awake.

'That's for you.' I open it. It's an application
for a house on camp. He tells me the best
ones to apply for, the ones closest to camp.

'I can come home then at lunchtime to see
you. I can take the kids to school and pick
them up. We can have a dog.'

'But I thought you didn't want me to come
now.'

'I never said that.' He looks shocked.

'You did, on Monday.' How could he have forgotten? It was only a few days ago.

'No, I didn't. Why would I not want you there? Have you changed your mind?' He looks like if I say yes he will be heartbroken.

'No.' My mind is going to explode with confusion. I don't know whether I am coming or going. I don't know if I should be happy that he has done a u-turn. I complete it over the weekend and he says he will hand it in first thing Monday so we can get a house sorted asap. He seems keen again for us to come. I am not so sure I feel the same.

22/04/2011

I have tried to ring Peter several times this morning to see if he has handed the form in, but I get no answer for ages. Finally, after the seventh attempt, he answers.

'I'm busy.'

'Oh right. I was just ringing to see if you handed in the form.'

'No. Will you just fucking leave me alone?'

'Fine.' I slam the phone down. This is ridiculous. He rings me straight back.

'Why did you put the phone down on me?' He is angry.

'Because you told me to leave you alone.'

'I didn't.'

'Do you know what, Peter, you are doing my head in. You just leave me alone.' I slam the phone down again and refuse to take his calls for the rest of the day. He texts me later that day to say he handed the application form in. I wish he hadn't. I have a really bad feeling that moving to camp would be the worst mistake ever, but I have accepted redundancy now. I can't turn back. I am stuck in a marriage I don't think I want anymore, but can't get out of.

14/05/2011

'Happy Birthday, Mummy.' My kids come in the bedroom with a sausage sandwich and a cup of tea. It's my fortieth birthday today. I am having a big party tonight. I have organised it all. Peter and the kids just have to make up the venue as a surprise. Not sure what kind of effort he will put in though. The house on camp is sorted now; will be ready for us to move in on 14th September, two weeks after I leave my job, so has fallen right. I say has fallen right, but it doesn't feel right. I am dreading it. Peter is so miserable and grumpy. He is snappy and nasty all the time; just downright horrible. He is verbally aggressive with me and the kids. His reprimands of them have started to worry me. I think he may go too far and hurt them. We have had loads of arguments where I have seen his face change to the monster I saw on Christmas Eve. When it happens I back off and take myself away from him as I fear what damage he will do to me this time. He seems then to take pleasure in having won the argument and will go out of his way to start another one as soon as he can. I don't answer back now, which is just not like me, but then I don't feel like me anymore. I try to convince myself it will all get better once we move, but deep down I know it is a terrible mistake and it will only get worse. But today is my birthday and I will put on my brave face in front of family and friends. No one will know the pain I am in and how my life is falling apart. Plus we go on holiday late tomorrow as well. I can't let things be ruined for the kids' sake and my brother and sister as we are going on holiday with them.

15/05/2011

Last night was good. I really enjoyed it. All my family were there and my friends. Peter and the kids did a good job on the venue. I said it looked great, but he just told me I was so ungrateful as I clearly didn't like it. Apparently the kids and my friends did most of it anyway; he kept disappearing. I can't win. It doesn't matter what I say. Thankfully he stood at the bar all night with his dad and left me alone to enjoy my night with those that care. So two-faced he looked laughing and joking with his dad. The man that he always said he hated so much and never wanted to be like now appears to be his best friend. I really wanted to have a go at him, but didn't through fear of what might happen. We are on the minibus to the airport. He is sat at the front talking to my brother and brother-in-law. He is animated when talking to them, holding court, he likes being the centre of attention. He flicks me the odd look now and again, as if to say 'are you still here?' I don't think this holiday is going to go well.

18/05/2011

We are on that rollercoaster again. One minute he is holding my hand and playing with the kids in the pool, then he is shouting at me in the street in front of everyone and telling the kids to go away and leave him alone. I have already sent him back to our room one night so he didn't ruin it for everyone. My family don't comment, but I can see they are embarrassed and don't know whether to step in. It's the Lanzarote Ironman triathlon contest today. The atmosphere at the resort is amazing. Maybe it will rub off on Peter. We are right at the finishing line so can cheer everyone coming in. Our hands hurt from clapping. The kids are loving high-fiving the sweaty runners as they come past.

'You could do this,' my sister suggests to Peter.

'Piece of piss. I would walk it.'

'Why don't you do it with John next year?'

'I'm up for it, if the old man can keep up with me.' John just laughs.

The rest of the night is good. The last of the finishing runners come in around midnight. We walk back to our hotel, clapping the last of the stragglers in. Peter is holding my hand and we are walking ahead of the others. From behind us our hands are pulled apart as Rebecca jumps in the middle. She gets embarrassed to see us showing affection. Peter grabs her by the arm and shakes her.

'You little bitch. Why do you always do that? Do you want me and your mum to split up?'

'Don't talk to her like that!' I protect my cowering daughter in my arms.

'You always stick up for her. She is a little bitch. She is trying to come between us.' With that he lunges at her again. She screams and cowers further under my arms.

'Calm down, Peter.' My brother has caught up with us.

'This is all her fault.' With that he storms off back to the room on his own for a second night.

19/05/2011

I wake and Peter is not there. I am so glad. I don't want to go over what happened last night. I get the kids up and we join the others by the pool. Peter appears at dinnertime.

'Where have you been?' He seems really excited and has a handful of papers. He sits on my sun bed.

'Look, babe. I have an entry form for next year's Ironman. I've been talking to the organisers and they have given me all the details of what I will need.' He gives me a detailed list of equipment he would need to take part; approximately £5,000's worth of equipment.

'We can't afford it.'

He has already put us in loads of debt with his spending. That is part of the reason for taking redundancy, to pay the debt off with my redundancy payment. He snatches the papers out of my hands.

'You can't tell me what to do. I'll do what I want.'

The rest of the holiday is pretty much a repeat of the last two days, but progressively worse. He is obsessed now with doing the Ironman. I am so worried. We have a joint bank account and I can't stop him spending money. When I try to tell him politely or otherwise I just get shouted down. He doesn't care who is there. We can't even get through one day without him kicking off with me and the kids. I don't know what I would do if my family weren't here. They comment that they have never seen him behave like this. Added to this, we get the news from home that my nan is in hospital and it doesn't look good. In fact, the best we can hope for is that she can hold out till we get home. Peter shows little interest or compassion though; the Ironman contest has taken over his every thought. The holiday was a total nightmare.

05/06/2011

We have been back from holiday a week now and nothing has changed. Thankfully my nan held out for us. I have been to see her a few times and I am going back today. Peter asks if he can come as he won't be home for a month now and it will probably be the last time he can see her before the inevitable. I reluctantly say yes. The last thing my nan needs is us arguing in front of her. We get to the ward and to the bay my nan is in; it's only her and a little old nun in the bed in the corner, although the nun is better and is sitting in the chair reading. She looks up as we enter and smiles. Peter stops.

'You go in. I will be back in a minute.' I go to my nan and sit with her for about ten minutes alone before Peter joins me. My nan hasn't said much, but when she sees Peter she perks up.

'Hello, Peter.' She always liked him. Liked him because he loved me. Little did she know the way he had been treating me, but now is not the time or the place. I sit back and leave them to their conversation. It's good to just see her speaking, even if it's strained and she keeps repeating herself. We only stay for about thirty minutes in total as she is tired and falls asleep.

06/06/2011

My phone beeps. It's my mum. The text has only three words in it, but they are the three words I have been dreading but expecting.

'Nan has gone.'

I don't text her back or ring her. Instead I automatically ring the person I want to be comforted by: Peter.

'What's up?'

'She's gone. My nan, she's died.'

'Why you telling me? She wasn't my Nan.'

'I thought you would want to know.' He liked my nan.

'Why would I? It's not my fault she died. I have to go, I'm at work.' The phone goes dead.

Surprisingly I don't feel stunned by his odd comments or even hurt. He makes a lot of them and I am used to his nastiness. I have given up trying to make sense of what he says. The tears begin to flow. Not for him, but for my lovely beautiful nan. I go and tell the kids and all three of us comfort each other. I realise Rebecca and Daniel are my comfort and have been for the last fifteen months.

01/07/2011

Peter was supposed to be home this weekend, but he rang to tell me he was going on a stag do on Saturday so wouldn't be coming home. He didn't just tell me, he said I can't stop him. The usual rant. I didn't even get a chance to open my mouth. This was just another example of him behaving differently. He used to live for the weekends and getting home to us. He turned down loads of chances to go on stag dos or nights out so he could come home. He would drink heavily as well on these nights out now, again not like him. To be honest, though, I was glad he wasn't coming home; these last few weeks without him have been great. Just me and the kids. Despite the fact we buried my nan, we have had a fun, relaxed time. It has made me realise how miserable and downtrodden Peter has made us and that we could be happy without him. But the impending move to camp is looming. I wish I could turn the clock back and take back my redundancy application. If I had known things were going to get this bad, I never would have put it in. I have resigned myself to the move and I will make the most of it. I have been looking at doing an Open University Degree. I have always wanted to do that, but never had the time. The kids and I have even been to look at some puppies to buy to take with us. They were so cute that we had to buy not one but two; a black one for Daniel and a golden one for Rebecca. We pick them up at the end of August.

12/08/2011

Peter is due home any minute. His visits have been sporadic over the last six weeks, but he is on leave now for three weeks. His behaviour has become even more out of hand. I don't recognise the man I once knew and loved. In fact, if I am honest, I don't love him anymore. In his own words he said he had become a monster and I agree. We have barely spoken recently. When we do, he tells me I don't know him anymore and I don't know what is going on in his head. I tell him to see the doctor, but he just tells me he will sort it out himself, after all he is not mad. I am not too sure on that one. He has rung today though, saying he is looking forward to us moving. One minute he cares, the next he doesn't. Right on cue he comes home. I am sat in the kitchen. As expected he doesn't look at me. Hardly talks to me. When I speak I just get snapped at. That's it, I have had enough.

'I can't do this anymore. I am not moving with you. I can't live with you like this. You've changed so much. I'm sorry, but I don't love you anymore. Just get your stuff and leave.'

He seems to take it on the chin.

'That's fine by me.' He goes upstairs to pack. The kids come down.

'Is Dad leaving?'

'Yes.'

'Good.' *Well, that was easy*, I think. But I spoke to soon. I hear him running back downstairs.

'She is kicking me out.' He comes over to me, sobbing and begging.

'Please don't do this. Don't leave me. I love you. I can't live without you. You don't know what is going on in my head. I need help.'

'I suggest you get it then, but in the meantime we're over.' He looks and sounds like my Peter, but as quickly as he was there, he is gone and the monster is back.

'I need to get out of this relationship before it destroys me.'

'You destroyed it. I'm stronger now, ready to fight back. I won't cower away no matter what the outcome may be. 'You've turned into a monster. I should have left you the moment you hit me.'

'I didn't hit YOU. You don't understand what's going on.' I don't care what is going on. I can't be bothered arguing.

'Just get your stuff and go. Go to your nan's.'

He storms off upstairs and starts bringing things down and packing his car. Once he has got most things, he comes back in the room to me and the kids. He begs me again not to do this, he can't live without us, says he will get help. I tell him to let me know when he has, until then it's over. With that, the monster is back.

'You bitch! I will kill you for doing this.'

He doesn't frighten me anymore, so I stand up and push him out the house. I shut and lock the door behind him and go back to Rebecca and Daniel. They come and comfort me.

'You have done the right thing, Mum. He scares us.'

I hadn't realised how grown up my two children had become. I hadn't realised what they had been going through and having to deal with. I hadn't realised what Peter had been doing to them when I wasn't there, but they were about to tell me.

When he looked after them he wouldn't feed them. He would go to McDonald's every day and make them watch him eat. Refused to buy them any food. They would steal bits of food when he went to the toilet. They were scared he would notice when he came back. People would watch and point at them.

If they were in his car, he would drive fast and swerve onto the opposite side of the road laughing that they were going to crash and die.

In the mornings, he would shout at them like squaddies to get up. Then he would go back to bed and leave them alone for the day, only getting up before I returned.

If he was angry in the car, he would flick off their seatbelts and tell them to get out when it was moving or he would pull up in the street, blocking traffic and try and drag them out.

One time with Rebecca in the car on the motorway, it was dark and he pulled up on the hard shoulder. He told her to get out and come and look at the licence plate. She did so and as she did he got back in and drove off down the hard shoulder. He stopped a little distance away. She was terrified and had to run after the car to get back in. He just said sorry, forgot she was there.

He would pack their bags and tell them they had to leave, that we didn't want them.

He would try and throw them out of the house. They would cling to the radiators and floor, scraping their nails along the carpet as he dragged them with their legs.

He would sit constantly on his phone texting his colleagues. They saw some of his texts, saying 'civilians will never understand what we have been through' or 'we need to stick together'.

How did I not know? How could I have left my children alone with this monster? How bad a mum am I? I feel so guilty.

13/08/2011

I wake up and switch my phone back on. I had to turn it off in the middle of the night. Peter was constantly texting and ringing, crying and begging me still to move with him, again saying he would get help. He would do anything to keep us. I stood my ground. Especially after what the kids had told me last night. He has clearly lost the plot and needs help. I did agree he could come back today to get the rest of his stuff.

He arrives around 16:00, two hours later than I told him to come. The kids let him in and he goes upstairs and gets the rest of his stuff. When he is finished he comes in the room and reaches for my chin to kiss me. I push his hand away. He looks like I have just cut his heart out with a knife.

'Why are you being like this? What have I done to deserve this?'

I let rip. I go through everything he has done: aggression, both verbal and physical; nastiness; not coming home; paranoia; heartlessness; pushing us away; not spending time with the kids; not talking to me and not even looking at me; no emotions; the holidays; my nan; Christmas; what he has done to the kids, etc.

'You don't know what it's like. What's going on in my head. In here [he jabs his head with his finger]. You wouldn't understand. No one can understand.'

He suddenly breaks down. He is crying, shaking, pacing. He's agitated, lost and he is scaring us again.

'STOP! For God's sake, what's wrong with you?'

He sits down and finally, after eighteen months of hell, he tells us exactly what's wrong with him.

'I can't look at you because I see them [Taliban] all the time. They are next to you. They are laughing at me. They say they are going to slit your throat. They come into the bedroom at night and stand by you. Pointing at you and running their fingers across your throat. That's why I pull you towards me. They were there when I was on R&R, pulling at my leg and pointing at you.

They were there yesterday when I got back. They are here now. When I speak to you on the phone they whisper in my ear. Telling me I don't deserve you because of what I did to them. It's them I shout at to leave me alone. That's why I don't answer the phone. I am there, but I can't speak to you because of them. I see them in my car when I drive home. I have to keep pulling up on the hard shoulder to tell them to stop. That's why I am late home. I go back early when it's light so I don't see them as much or I don't come home at all. I stay at camp or go out with the lads and get drunk to get rid of them. But they come in my room. The lock doesn't stop them. They tell me I'm worthless. I don't deserve to live. It was my fault Green died. It should have been me. That's why I stay at work till late, so I don't have to go to my room. It was my fault your nan died. They were there when we visited her. They wouldn't come in the room because of the nun. That's why I hung back. They were there at the Summer Ball. I didn't have work to do. I went back to my room to keep them away from you. Disappeared when you were talking to Clarky because they were tormenting me. I see them in my car. In the back, between the kids. They tell me I don't deserve them, that I should smash the car into the wall and kill us all. That you are better off without me anyway. I nearly did it once, with you and the kids in the car. On holiday they were there telling me not to let you dictate to me about the Ironman contest. That Rebecca was trying to split us up. That she is a spy. Spying on me all the time. That the kids hate me anyway. I can't play with Daniel because when I do, I see him blow up in front of me like the boy in Afghanistan. They tell me that he is the boy that tried to kill us and that I should kill him first. I should slit his throat. They slit his throat in front of me all the time.'

With that he grabs Daniel by the hair, pulls his neck back and slices his finger across his throat to demonstrate what he sees. Daniel is visibly shaken.

'I have nightmares about them, about Green and Smith. I blame myself for their deaths, it was my fault. I have flashbacks all the time. In Greece I didn't get up early to put towels down. I got up when the planes came in. I thought I was back in Afghanistan. I first saw them in Afghanistan. It was true what the others said about me. They were there then. They followed me home. They followed me into the hall when I first saw you. Worst of all I see them after I killed them. They have bullet holes in their heads, bits missing and blood pouring down. That's why I got moved. I kept seeing them. I kept trying to kill them over and over again, but they wouldn't die. I never hit you at Christmas. I would never hurt you. I hit them. It wasn't your face I saw, it was theirs. I told the police that. I have to get away from you all before I hurt you. You deserve better than me. You are all better off without me. I love you, but I can't be around you. They won't leave me alone if I stay with you. There is only one way I can stop them.'

'STOP!' I've heard enough.

What he has just told us over the last hour was frightening. It's irrational. It's unimaginable. It's horrific. It's scary. It's barbaric. IT'S NOT REAL. It's clearly not real, but to him it is so very real and it's so obvious now, so very obvious. He has PTSD, on a massive scale. I don't feel scared; I feel relieved. As crazy as it all is, it makes sense to me, so much sense. It explains away the madness of these last eighteen months. He had clearly been to hell – in fact he's still there – but so had we. But now I have an answer. I know why we have been living through a nightmare. He is on his knees now. His head is in my lap. He is holding my hands. He is still shaking and sobbing uncontrollably.

'I'm begging you, Peter, get help. You're ill. We will be here for you. We will help you. You've been injured, invisibly injured. You need treatment, psychological treatment.'

With that he is gone again and the monster returns. He throws my hands away. The tears and the shaking abruptly stop.

'I need to get away from you before I go insane.' With that he goes to his car and he is gone.

Chapter 9 – PTSD

19/08/2011

This week has been the worst week of my life. I have been to the doctors' and got a sick note to sign me off until the end of August. I don't even have the time to worry about the fact that I am now jobless, with a mortgage to pay. Peter claims to have seen the doctor himself as he feels like he can't breathe. He wakes up in the night sweating and feeling like he is having a heart attack. The doctor supposedly told him he is suffering from anxiety. The begging for forgiveness has continued, together with the threats to kill himself. He has been to see the kids, but doesn't stay long if he turns up at all. When he does, he just follows me round like a lap dog; doesn't go near the kids. He storms off when I mention PTSD.

Today has been particularly bad. He has sent texts all day saying if I don't take him back, he will end it all. He rings as well and puts thoughts in my mind that I don't want to think.

'This is all the kids' fault. We would be happy if they weren't here. I wish we had never had them. I wish they were out the way.'

Clearly the voices in his head are becoming more vindictive. I decide the kids are not to be left alone with him again. The threats continue all day. He rings me up to tell me he is going to end it all tomorrow.

'You are all better off without me. I am just going to go away tomorrow and end it all. I can't handle it.' It's a three-way conversation as he argues with the demons whispering in his ear. 'Fuck off and leave me alone, will you?'

'Are they talking to you now?' This is the first time I have heard him talking to them. Although in hindsight I now realise this has happened plenty of times in the last eighteen months, when our phone conversations made no sense at all as he was talking to the voices in his head at the same time as talking to me.

'Yes. I am going to stop all this.' He sounds deadly serious this time about killing himself.

20/08/2011

I have been up all night. I couldn't sleep. I know him well enough to know that his threats to kill himself are serious. I don't know whether to tell his family and the army or not. They know nothing of what has gone on. My family do. I call my mum and ask what I should do. If I don't tell them and he does do something, they will hate me for not telling them everything. It will be my fault. He has begged me not to tell them and I promised I wouldn't, but I don't know that I can stick to my promise.

My mum says I should ring the Army Welfare Service (AWS) for advice and ring his nan up. I haven't spoken to her since I kicked him out. We always got along well. I at least owe her the truth. I ring and she answers straight away. I tell her everything he told us last week; how he has threatened to kill himself; and what he said last night. She listens in silence before she shoves the knife in my back.

'You're lying. He just doesn't want to be with you anymore.'

As I feel the metaphorical pain of the knife, I continue. I tell her I am going to ring the AWS and tell them exactly what I have told her.

'Just leave him alone. I will talk to him.' With that the phone goes dead. A minute later it rings; it's Peter and I am subjected to a tirade of abuse.

'You are a pain in my arse. I want to get away from you. Why won't you get the message that I don't love you? Leave me alone. This has nothing to do with the army.' Twisting the knife further I hear his nan in the background.

'Put the phone down on her. Ring the army up yourself and tell them about HER.'

I stay quite calm, despite the furore of abuse I am getting from the other end of the phone. I tell Peter calmly that he needs to get help and if he doesn't ring the AWS up himself in the next hour I will. With that I put the phone down as I continue to hear the tirade coming from both him and his nan. Ten seconds later my phone beeps; it's Peter.

'Babe, please don't do this, I love you.' I laugh. Ten seconds ago I was a pain in his arse. For the next hour I am bombarded with these messages. I don't answer until the hour is up. I send him one message.

'You clearly have not rung, so I am ringing the AWS now.' I have the number to hand and ring. I explain my situation. They ask for some details: his regimental number; his regiment; when he was in Afghanistan; what he has been doing/saying; how long this has been going on, etc. They are very helpful. They acknowledge that he clearly has PTSD or Combat Stress as they refer to it. They seem very sympathetic and I think they will be able to help, until they say they have it recorded but they can't do anything unless he rings them. What a complete waste of time. There is no way he is going to ring the army and tell them; they will think him weak. For the next hour I continue to be bombarded with texts from Peter wanting to know what they said. After an hour I blackmail him by saying that if he doesn't ring them in the next ten minutes they will ring his CO. My phone goes silent. Ten minutes later it rings. It's the AWS. He has rung. He told them he was perfectly fine. They offer me advice on how to get a divorce and claim child maintenance. Clearly he had spouted the same crap he told his nan and they believed it. So much for the army looking after the families. I didn't need divorce advice; I needed help to save my husband from destroying everything we had. That's it. I'm done trying to help him. I continue to get the begging texts and phone calls from him, but I ignore them all.

14/09/2011

It's been nearly a month now since I have physically spoken to Peter. He texts me constantly and rings on unknown numbers to try and get me to answer. I am seriously not interested. I have bigger things to worry about like getting a job. I am living off my redundancy at the moment. The only text I send him is to say I want a divorce and to tell him how much he should pay in terms of child maintenance. I went on the CSA website and worked it out correctly. He offered to pay half, said he has been told it was 'the going rate'. It was probably his Taliban friends who control his life who told him. Going rate, what are they, a couple of hookers he is paying the going rate for? I told him he either pays what the CSA website says or we take it to court as part of the divorce. The threat of court makes him agree. He knows the truth will come out in court and the army will find out about his PTSD.

He wants to meet on the 17th at Meadowhall so he can buy Daniel a birthday present. I would rather not, but it's not about me. We have at least agreed he will come and visit the kids every two weeks, although he has yet to turn up. He promises them he will come on Friday to see them. I have a job interview on the 16th. Should be a given. It's pretty much my old job. If my financial situation is sorted then that will be one less thing to worry about.

16/09/2011

Devastated. I didn't get the job. I was so sure. How could I not? It was my old job. My old boss rang. Patronising cow with her sympathetic 'ring me if you want to talk about it' tone. I am gutted. What am I going to do? The money from Peter doesn't even cover the mortgage. I have my redundancy, but that won't last forever. I am going to have to sign on. How embarrassing. No surprise as well, Peter didn't turn up to see the kids. They were so upset. Kept asking when he would be here and he never came. They were so angry; said they didn't want to see him again.

17/09/2011

My phone rings; it's Peter. *Here we go*, I think: excuses.

'What time we meeting?'

'We're not.' Cheeky get. Is he taking the piss? He doesn't turn up to see the kids when promised and then rings the next day as if nothing is wrong.

'I forgot I said I would come.' Not good enough as far as I am concerned, but Daniel wants to go so he can get a present. He's not bothered about seeing Peter, just wants a present. He is still only seven after all. So I reluctantly agree.

We go to my mum's first. I am still so upset by not getting the job. Really worried about what I am going to do about money. I am really teary. I know Peter will try to hold my hand, kiss me and act like we are a couple. I seriously don't think I can handle it. I walk into my mum's and instantly burst out crying. This is the first time she has seen me break.

'I can't do it anymore, Mum. I can't put on a brave face. I hate him for what he has done. I want to kill him for wrecking everything. He won't care. He will try to act like we are still a couple. All I want to do is smash his face in for this.'

'Don't go, Kathryn. It's not fair what this is doing to you.' My mum is seriously concerned for me.

'How can I not? It's about Daniel, not me. I can't let Daniel down. I have to go.' I make the excuse I am just upset over not getting the job and I will be fine.

We meet Peter at the shopping centre, late as usual. The hallucinations still haunting and delaying him obviously. As I suspect, straight away he attempts to hold my hand and I pull away. I can't even look at him. I just want to hurry up. We walk round for ages before Daniel settles on a skateboard. Peter pays and we go to our cars.

'Can Dad come and watch me on the skateboard?'

'Dad has to go.' I don't want him to come.

'No, I don't.' Now he wants to see them.

'Please, Mummy.' This is a nightmare. I just want to get home away from him. But I agree.

'Do you want to come in my car?'

'NO. We will go with Mummy.' No way are they going in his car, alone with him.

We get back and Peter arrives behind us. He doesn't go outside to watch Daniel as promised, he follows me inside. I go down to the kitchen, but he follows me. I really don't need this. I am on the edge emotionally. I am struggling to hold back the tears. I sit at the table and he sits next to me and takes my hands. I pull them away. He reaches for my chin and I move it out the way.

'Why won't you look at me?'

'I can't. You're not you.'

'I am. Please look at me.' He grabs my chin and turns my face to his. I can't stop them, the tears; they tumble like a torrential rainfall. 'Why are you crying?'

'Because you're not you.'

'I am. I'm still in here. I'm just lost. Lost in Afghanistan. I need to process what happened. I need to file it so I can get back to you. I have seen a doctor and I am starting a counselling course with the Royal British Legion. I will sort this. I promise. I know I need help. Your tears mean nothing to me.' Well that didn't help. The storm clouds kick in and I am sobbing. He lifts my head again to look at him. He looks me dead in the eyes.

'Don't you see? You being upset means nothing to me. You are invisible to me. I have to block you out to protect myself. I need to sort myself out before I can sort us out. Please don't leave me. I will sort this. I swear.' He takes my chin in his hand again and kisses me. HE kisses me, my Peter, not the monster. He looks me dead in the eyes again.

'Life without you is not worth living. I have never stopped loving you and I always will. I will come back to you no matter how long it takes. You just have to give me time. Promise me you will wait for me, no matter what.' I nod. He seems so genuine, he must be telling the truth about the counselling.

10/10/2011

It's been three weeks since Peter said he was getting counselling. In fairness he has kept in touch during the week, telling me about the counselling and we seem to be turning a corner. But PTSD is such a tease. It allows you only glimpses of the one you love, constantly throwing you sticks to make you think your loved one is coming back to you, but then it knocks you down again. Back down to earth with a bang. The sticks get smaller and the thuds as you hit the ground get louder. He rings during the week, but nothing at weekends. He says it's because he has to go to Salisbury for the course as it's the closest. He can't ring till Monday. Nonsense, I know he lied about the course. Just read up about PTSD online. I had too, done nothing but for the last two months. I found a brilliant site called the Big White Wall. They have talkabouts on there, the odd one from squaddies suffering from PTSD who have acted in the same way as Peter. I switched my phone off last night. I knew, as it was Monday, he would call, especially as it's his birthday. I switch it back on and it rings straight away. It's not him but my mum, so I answer.

'Peter has rung me. He wants to know where you are. He is in a state. He says he has found a woman hanging from a tree on the course he is on. He sounds so depressed. It's his birthday too and no one has sent him a card.' My mum knows he is lying. She knows how ill he is. She asks me to ring him anyway. She is worried for him. They had a great relationship. He used to call her 'Mum', said she was more of a mum to him than either his real mum or his stepmum. Despite all he has done to me, my mum is still worried sick about him. I ring. He tells me a slightly different story.

He found someone hanging from the fire escape. He called an ambulance. They took her away, end of story. He is clearly getting worse. I challenge him about even being on a course. He insists he is at first, but after arguing with me for an hour he admits he lied just to shut me up. There is no course with the Royal British Legion.

'So why make up such an outrageous story like finding someone hanging on a course you are not even doing?'

'I did. I did find someone hanging.' He is so convinced he would probably pass a lie detector test. Through my research into PTSD I realise his mind is so shattered and jumbled he has probably seen someone hanging in Afghanistan and is having flashbacks and thinks it's real now. I tell him my theory.

'You're my wife not my fucking counsellor.' The monster returns.

19/12/2011

The kids and I are at Butlins. The holiday had been booked for a year. Peter was meant to come. But me and the kids are looking forward to it. We have only been here half an hour when Daniel is so busy running around he trips and cracks his head open. I try and stop the bleeding, but my hands are covered in blood. We are rushed to the hospital so he can get sorted. I text Peter immediately, but it takes him three days to call and check on him.

25/12/2011

Christmas Day. No phone calls from Peter to the kids to wish them Happy Christmas. I have no desire to talk to him and have deleted his phone number. I bought Rebecca her own phone. He promised to ring her every day. But has not rung yet.

15/03/2012

Since Christmas, Peter's visits to the kids have become nonexistent. The kids could not care less and I have given up trying to get him to stick to our agreement. He hasn't kept to his promise to ring Rebecca every day, which has broken her heart. She wrote to him every day in Afghanistan and he can't be bothered to return the favour. He is coming today to see them though before he goes to Brunei. I don't believe for one second he is going anywhere. It's an excuse not to see them. Surprisingly, he arrives on time and we all sit in the kitchen. Peter launches into his usual remorse. He tells Rebecca his phone is broken, that's why he could not ring. He tells her how much he loves her, loves me, he will never love anyone else, etc., he is ill and he will sort this. He then receives a text message and answers it; they continue back and forth. I ask who it is.

'I am supposed to be going on a date tomorrow. My mate is sorting it. But I won't go because she's not you.' Rebecca is heartbroken and confused after what he said only a minute ago. This is nothing short of emotional abuse. He turns to Daniel.

'Do you understand what's wrong with me?'

'You're mental.' With that Peter jumps from the table and lunges at him. Daniel jumps back in fear. I realise he is next to the knife drawer. I manage to get in the way, between Peter and Daniel. The monster is now towering above me fists at the ready, ready to strike, just like on Christmas Eve. This time I play my trump card.

'You dare and I will have you kicked out of the army quicker than you can say your name.' I lock eyes with the monster. They are wide and transfixed for what seems like an age. They flicker and he pulls back.

'I can't do this anymore.' He goes to the door and leaves. We watch his car go up the hill and then it stops. My phone rings. It's him.

'I can't do this anymore.' He's crying. 'I'm going to hurt them or you. I don't know what I am doing.'

I know that this has to stop.

'Enough now. You need to stay away from us. We are not safe around you. If you come near us again without getting help, I will get a court order to stop you.' He promises to stay away. Away from us and away from Sheffield.

21/04/2012

It's a week after Rebecca's tenth birthday. She received no card and no phone call from her dad. But tonight he rings. I refuse to speak to him, so she does. She is so brave, she gives him what for. Tells him herself she does not want him to ring her ever again. She gives me the phone. I don't give him the chance to talk or make excuses.

'Enough is enough now. No random phone calls. No visits. No contact. You are dead to us and you have been for a very long time. The divorce is with the solicitor. You don't need to speak to me. Leave the kids alone. Don't ever contact us again. This is done now, once and for all.'

18/07/2012

I have another job interview today. I have had loads and got turned down. The redundancy money will only last till the end of August. I feel like I have let my kids down. I really don't know what I will do when the money's gone. I fear we will lose the house. I have kind of given up the fight. I go to the interview thinking what the heck, if I am not right for you, then you're not right for me. But miracles do happen; I get the job. This massive weight on my shoulders has finally been lifted.

01/08/2012

I have spent a lot of time this last year researching PTSD. Not to help Peter, but to help myself and the children understand the nightmare we have been through. I am not one for counselling, but found one site a great source of comfort: the Big White Wall. The site is specifically for people experiencing mental health issues, either their own or others'. They have talkabouts that you can get involved in. I registered on there in the midst of all the madness, but have yet to make a posting. But today a new talkabout catches my eye. 'Help, serving husband PTSD.' It was started by an army wife whose husband has been acting strangely, leaving home, disappearing for days, has started being aggressive with their child, he is a cold and miserable person. She asks if anyone else has been through the same. I watch this talkabout for a few weeks, her interactions with the Wall Guide (the online counsellors). She is joined by an ex-forces guy who has suffered from PTSD; he explains how they don't talk to their loved ones, how they feel ugly inside for what they have seen and done.

23/08/2012

This woman is just embarking on her nightmare and I feel the need to let her know she is not alone. So I make a post:

'After ten years of marriage and a six-month tour of Afghanistan my soul mate and love of my life deteriorated rapidly from a loving and dedicated husband and father into a violent and miserable monster. He used to live for the weekends till he returned home; this changed and he would make excuses not to come; when he was here our weekends were miserable. I thought he may be having an affair, but throughout he swore his love for me and would never do this. It came to a head when he broke down in front of me and the children, crying hysterically that he was hearing voices, hallucinating, having nightmares. He was suicidal. He said and did much more that was terrifying. He became dangerous to be around. We begged him to get help, but to no avail; he wouldn't for fear of being deemed weak. The army were of no help. Visits were sporadic, nasty and aggressive. He pushed us away and we no longer have contact; our divorce will be finalised within weeks. The man we loved

died on the fields of Afghanistan, but we had to watch it happen. It would have been easier had he been killed by an IED or a sniper's bullet. We would still be entitled to our happy memories, but they have been stolen from us. We are left with memories of a monster that turned our lives upside down.

We have grieved for the man we loved and lost and have spent eighteen months of hell living with the monster who returned in his place. Not until the moment myself and the kids said enough is enough and walked away could we rebuild our shattered lives.

So you are not alone and I promise there is light at the end of the tunnel.

All the best.'

Later that night I log on again to see if she has read my story. She hasn't yet, but the Wall Guide has responded to me. What I read is immensely difficult, so heartbreaking in its honesty, so tragic in its finality, but so reassuring in its diagnosis:

'To watch as the person you loved and who loved you back become a source of pain for you, your children and himself must have been difficult.

The day he broke down and showed himself lost, confused and suffering must have been terrifying, but maybe it was his way of saying goodbye, so you will know that it wasn't him but the monster inside that was directing its anger at you and the kids; that by pushing you away he is protecting you from his darkness, as it is something that has overpowered and destroyed the man he was.

You can only help those who want to be helped, you can only support the ones who will accept the support, you can love no matter what – but you can't save those that don't want to be saved.'

My resolve is totally smashed. I have held it together so well up till now. I read the piece over and over again. I hadn't realised but my tears are flowing. It was so brutally honest that, whilst devastating to read, it was also so comforting.

05/09/2012

I continue to log on and post on the talkabout on a daily basis; over the weeks, many more wives, girlfriends, partners, mums and soldiers join the discussion. I realise my situation is in no way unique, it just has never been talked about before. The code of silence.

The posts from the guys suffering or who have suffered from PTSD acknowledge that whilst they sat protected in their emotionless bubbles, they had subjected their loved ones to traumas far beyond what they were going through.

PTSD is clearly a global issue. A wife joins the discussion from Australia. Her story is uncanny in how it mirrors mine. But she is in a dark and bad place. She is still in the midst of the madness and is struggling to find her way out. She clearly is contemplating ending her pain in the most dramatic and final of ways. We band together and help her through it. Help her find her way through the fog. We are her virtual shoulder to cry on. Thankfully, she manages to get herself together.

05/10/2012

Our band of merry men and women continues to grow over the month. Each member at different stages of their story. Fortunately, there is always someone there to guide them and hold their hand through to the next chapter. No matter how difficult that chapter will be. We even have developed our own motto: 'KEEP FIGHTING AND STAY STRONG.' Tragically, there are more women and children suffering violence and aggression at the hands of their loved ones. More thoughts and attempts at suicide. Whilst every new story is tragic and heartbreaking, there is comfort to be had in knowing that we are not alone in going through or having been through the horrors of loving someone with PTSD.

I feel that having survived the ordeal I am in a good place to console and offer advice. But today is a day I cry out for the support of my virtual friends. My divorce came through today. I am beyond heartbroken. Even till the end I hoped he would stop this tragedy. He has rung often enough to say he will. The pain of your heart breaking is a real physical pain. I can't physically speak, so I post on BWW the simple words:

'GUTTED!!!!! Divorce came through today.'

My beautiful and inspirational virtual shoulders to cry on come up trumps. They are there like a shot and sit beside me through one more of the dips on this rollercoaster ride of emotions. Fortunately, I am no longer blindfolded or alone on this ride and they hold my hand until it's over and I can get off for good.

I realise, whilst I have always said I am not one for counselling, that the BWW and my friends on the talkabout are my counsellors and amazing ones at that.

15/03/2013

It's been a year now since we have physically seen Peter. I still get the odd phone call. The promises. But it's clear his demons are still with him. Whilst he still professes his undying love for me, he has a new girlfriend and did commit the ultimate betrayal of our marriage. Thankfully, whilst the monster still haunts me, I have no feelings or emotions for him, so he no longer hurts me.

The year has not been without PTSD rearing its ugly head. Rebecca struggled emotionally. Her anger and frustration was taken out on me, Daniel and her school friends. Thankfully, with help from the school, we guided her through her emotions and anger. I am so proud of her and Daniel for being so brave in coping with what they have.

To this day Peter has never acknowledged what he did to us or told anyone else what he told us. I have no idea how much of what he said was true or just his broken mind playing tricks on him. He has never been officially diagnosed with PTSD, so we carry this heavy burden alone.

04/08/2013

Sadly I have no romantic ending to tell. I wish I could write about how Peter won his battle with PTSD and how we are now blissfully back together as the happy family we once were. But PTSD rarely allows you the happy ending you fight so hard for.

PTSD is cruel. It deprived me of my happy memories, stole them from me and refused to give them back without a battle. I lost that battle and I am left alone, with only memories of anger and heartbreak.

PTSD stole my children's memories of the man they once loved and adored, and has left them only with memories of fear and rejection. PTSD stole from them the memories of the daddy who made them feel safe and has left them with memories of a man who hurt them. PTSD stole the man that was their hero.

My story is not unique; the Big White Wall is testament to that. The tragedy is we are just the ones that put our heads above the wire. PTSD will continue to be surrounded by a code of silence. PTSD will continue to be hidden for fear of being considered weak. PTSD will continue to take lives and this will continue to break hearts. PTSD will continue to leave people broken.

The only way to break this silence is to talk and write about how things really are. More of us should tell our stories.

My happy ending is that I survived PTSD. I am in a very happy place and life is great. Kids are fabulous. Work is good. Finances are sorted. Even romance is on the horizon.

Rebecca, Daniel and I have and continue to make new memories. PTSD no longer lurks around the corner ready to pounce and steal them away.

PTSD may have won the battle, but I won the fight.

ACKNOWLEDGEMENTS

My family, friends, colleagues and neighbours.

For all your love and support through the good times and the tough times.

My mum.

For holding me up when I had fallen.

For encouraging and reminding me of how strong I am.

Rebecca and Daniel.

For holding the pieces together when I was broken.

For being so strong and brave.

For giving me so many memories, both old and new.

For being my life and my world.

I love you both.